# UTAH TRIVIA

# UTAH TRIVIA

COMPILED BY ALLAN KENT POWELL AND
MIRIAM B. MURPHY

Rutledge Hill Press®
*Nashville, Tennessee*

Published by Rutledge Hill Press, a Division of Thomas Nelson Inc., P.O.Box 141000, Nashville, Tennessee 37214.

Typography by D&T/Bailey Typesetting, Inc., Nashville, Tennessee.

**Library of Congress Cataloging-in-Publication Data**

Utah trivia / compiled by Allan Kent Powell and Miriam B. Murphy.
    p.  cm.
    ISBN 1-55853-464-4
    1. Utah—Miscellanea.  I. Powell, Allan Kent.  II. Murphy,
Miriam B., 1933–
F826.U894   1997
979.2—dc21                            97-2995
                                       CIP

*Printed in the United States of America*
2  3  4  5  6  7  8  9  — 08  07  06  05  04

# PREFACE

It is with great pleasure that we bring you this book, *Utah Trivia*. It is designed to further educate and fascinate you by offering a wealth of historical and cultural information that tells the wonderful story of Utah. We who live in the Beehive State are proud of our state's accomplishments and contributions to society, and this book will be a source of hours of enjoyment for those who know and love Utah. Likewise, we believe that *Utah Trivia* contains many pearls of factual knowledge that will also intrigue and test those who live outside of Utah.

Although we put this book together in commemoration of the state's 1996 centennial and the 1997 sesquicentennial of the Mormon settlement of Utah, it is a book that appeals to all interests and backgrounds and is timeless in its sense of historical perspective.

Excuse us for sounding so provincial, but we believe that Utah is truly unique among our nation's fifty states for its combination of dramatic natural beauty, cultural diversity, and technological contributions. When many people foreign to our great state hear it mentioned, they conjure up such images as the Great Salt Lake, snow-capped mountain peaks, gigantic stone arches, and the Mormon Tabernacle Choir. What they don't realize is that Utah's deep historical significance also includes the distinction of being, literally, the meeting point for transcontinental rail and communications systems connecting the East and the West. But even that bit of knowledge is only the tip of the iceberg in what we are confident is a treat of a book for anyone looking to have fun while increasing his or her knowledge of Utah.

Enjoy.

—Allan Kent Powell and Miriam B. Murphy

To the wonderful people of the state of Utah

# TABLE OF CONTENTS

# GEOGRAPHY

**Q.** What town is named for John Hanselena, a Prussian miner and horse trader?

**A.** Dutch John.

◆

**Q.** In which three major physiographic provinces does Utah lie?

**A.** Basin and Range, Colorado Plateau, and Rocky Mountain.

◆

**Q.** For whom is the city of Ogden named?

**A.** Peter Skene Ogden (leader of a Hudson Bay fur-trapping brigade).

◆

**Q.** Approximately how many lakes are in the Uinta Mountains?

**A.** Fourteen hundred.

◆

**Q.** What city in the Sanpete Valley is named for the angel who showed Joseph Smith the golden plates from which the Book of Mormon was translated?

**A.** Moroni.

**Q.** What geographic entity is associated with the "bench" areas, which are popular with homeowners in the Salt Lake Valley because of their elevated views?

**A.** Lake Bonneville.

---

**Q.** For whom is the city of Saint George named?

**A.** George Albert Smith.

---

**Q.** What prominent fault runs through the most populated area of the state?

**A.** Wasatch.

---

**Q.** What county is named for the rich coal deposits found within its boundaries?

**A.** Carbon.

---

**Q.** What high mountain range separates Beaver and Piute Counties?

**A.** Tushar Mountains.

---

**Q.** Utah contains how many counties?

**A.** Twenty-nine.

---

**Q.** What is the highest mountain range in the Utah portion of the Great Basin?

**A.** Deep Creek Mountains.

**Q.** What gave Skull Valley in Tooele County its name?

**A.** Buffalo skulls found there in the 1850s.

———◆———

**Q.** What river connects Utah Lake and the Great Salt Lake?

**A.** Jordan.

———◆———

**Q.** What is the highest point in Utah?

**A.** Kings Peak (13,528 feet).

———◆———

**Q.** What city had passed Ogden in population by 1980?

**A.** Provo.

———◆———

**Q.** What ethnic minority is Utah's largest?

**A.** Hispanic.

———◆———

**Q.** Which county was created in 1880 from parts of Summit, Wasatch, and Sanpete Counties?

**A.** Uintah.

———◆———

**Q.** Which county has voted for Democratic candidates more often than any other?

**A.** Carbon.

**Q.** What is the lowest point in Utah?

**A.** Beaver Dam Wash (2,350 feet).

———◆———

**Q.** The area of Utah is how many square miles?

**A.** 84,916.

———◆———

**Q.** In area, what is Utah's rank among the fifty states?

**A.** Eleventh.

———◆———

**Q.** How many peaks in the Uinta Mountains are higher than thirteen thousand feet?

**A.** Twenty-four.

———◆———

**Q.** Which large suburb southeast of Salt Lake City was formerly a smelting and transportation hub for the mines in the nearby canyons?

**A.** Sandy.

———◆———

**Q.** What is the tallest mountain in the Wasatch Range?

**A.** Mount Nebo (11,877 feet).

———◆———

**Q.** What is the name of the ancient lake of which the Great Salt Lake is a remnant?

**A.** Lake Bonneville.

**Q.** Morgan County was named for whom?

**A.** Jedediah Morgan Grant.

---

**Q.** What was the last county created in Utah?

**A.** Daggett (1917).

---

**Q.** What are Utah's three most populous cities?

**A.** Salt Lake City, West Valley City, and Provo.

---

**Q.** Utah is bordered by what six states?

**A.** Idaho, Wyoming, Colorado, New Mexico, Arizona, and Nevada.

---

**Q.** Which two towns have only three letters in their names?

**A.** Loa and Roy.

---

**Q.** What is the largest Indian tribe in Utah?

**A.** Navajo.

---

**Q.** Early pioneers passed through which Wasatch Front canyon to enter the Salt Lake Valley?

**A.** Emigration.

**Q.** How many lakes are on Thousand Lake Mountain in Wayne County?

**A.** None (cartographers probably should have given that name to the neighboring Aquarius Plateau).

◆

**Q.** Interstates 80 and 15 intersect in what city?

**A.** Salt Lake City.

◆

**Q.** Utah contains how many national parks?

**A.** Five.

◆

**Q.** What railroad community, established in 1883, was destroyed one hundred years later by a massive mudslide that blocked rivers and flooded the town?

**A.** Thistle.

◆

**Q.** A railroad siding in Iron County was named for what famous author of westerns?

**A.** Zane Grey (Zane).

◆

**Q.** What Utah Lake resort was named for a famous New York resort?

**A.** Saratoga.

◆

**Q.** What is the largest national park in Utah?

**A.** Canyonlands (337,750 acres).

**Q.** What was the first east-west highway to cross Utah?

**A.** Lincoln Highway.

———◆———

**Q.** For whom was the town of Orangeville named?

**A.** Orange Seely.

———◆———

**Q.** Three Utah rivers—Duchesne, Price, and San Rafael—have what in common?

**A.** All are tributaries of the Green River.

———◆———

**Q.** What is unusual about Roosevelt's Union High School?

**A.** It straddles the boundary of Uintah and Duchesne Counties.

———◆———

**Q.** For what, not whom, was Nancy Patterson Canyon in San Juan County named?

**A.** A race horse.

———◆———

**Q.** What is the correct pronunciation of the county spelled J-u-a-b?

**A.** JOO-ab.

———◆———

**Q.** For which U.S. president was the city of Roosevelt named?

**A.** Theodore Roosevelt.

**Q.** What is the projected population of the state by the year 2020?

**A.** More than three million.

———◆———

**Q.** Which two Utah towns were renamed after donors of libraries to the communities?

**A.** Blanding (formerly Grayson) and Bicknell (formerly Thurber).

———◆———

**Q.** How do Utah's Uinta Mountains differ from most mountain ranges in North America?

**A.** They run east and west.

———◆———

**Q.** The former Mukuntuweap National Monument is now called by what name?

**A.** Zion National Park.

———◆———

**Q.** Utah's northern boundary lies along what parallel?

**A.** Forty-second.

———◆———

**Q.** What three states join Utah in forming the Four Corners, the only point in the United States where four states meet?

**A.** Arizona, Colorado, and New Mexico.

———◆———

**Q.** Which county and its seat are named for an American president?

**A.** Millard (county), Fillmore (county seat).

**Q.** With a twisting course of nearly five hundred miles, what river ends only ninety miles from its origin?

**A.** Bear.

———◆———

**Q.** What lake is divided almost equally between Utah and Idaho?

**A.** Bear Lake.

———◆———

**Q.** What is Utah's largest county?

**A.** San Juan (7,725 square miles).

———◆———

**Q.** The Uintah and Ouray Indian Reservation occupies land in what three counties?

**A.** Duchesne, Uintah, and Grand.

———◆———

**Q.** What is the elevation of the Great Salt Lake?

**A.** Forty-two hundred feet above sea level.

———◆———

**Q.** After Salt Lake County, what is Utah's most populous county?

**A.** Utah.

———◆———

**Q.** How much snow fell at Utah's highest ski resorts from November 1983 to April 1984?

**A.** 650 to 700 inches.

**Q.** What landmark was used on Utah's centennial license plate?

**A.** Delicate Arch.

———◆———

**Q.** What is the elevation of Hidden Peak at the top of the Snowbird Tram?

**A.** Eleven thousand feet.

———◆———

**Q.** The Green and Colorado Rivers form one boundary for which seven counties?

**A.** Carbon, Emery, Wayne, Grand, San Juan, Garfield, and Kane.

———◆———

**Q.** What was the name of Butch Cassidy's isolated hideout?

**A.** Robbers Roost.

———◆———

**Q.** A rich mining district was named for what Indian chief?

**A.** Tintic.

———◆———

**Q.** A total of 9.6 million acres of Utah land are currently classified for what purpose?

**A.** Farming.

———◆———

**Q.** What former coal mining camp was named using the four initials of the principal investors?

**A.** Mohrland (Mays, Orem, Heiner, Rice).

**Q.** Which five Indian tribes possess reservation lands in Utah?

**A.** Shoshone, Goshute, Piute, Utes, and Navajo.

———◆———

**Q.** In what canyon, through which I-80 now passes, did Mormon militiamen set up fortifications against the U.S. Army in 1857?

**A.** Echo.

———◆———

**Q.** What town was named for the extra engines put on trains there to assist in getting them over Soldier Summit?

**A.** Helper.

———◆———

**Q.** What is left of ancient Uinta Lake that was formed in the late Tertiary period?

**A.** The basin that held it, Uinta Basin.

———◆———

**Q.** Utah produced 88.5 million pounds of what kind of meat in 1993?

**A.** Turkey.

———◆———

**Q.** Which city is known as the Junction City because of its importance as a railroad crossroads?

**A.** Ogden.

———◆———

**Q.** What do the San Rafael Reef, Waterpocket Fold, and Comb Wash have in common?

**A.** All are ancient geological upthrusts.

**Q.** In which county is the mining town of Eureka situated?

**A.** Juab.

---

**Q.** Which nation claimed ownership of present-day Utah until 1848?

**A.** Mexico.

---

**Q.** What city was the uranium boom capital of Utah in the 1950s?

**A.** Moab.

---

**Q.** When it was established in 1980, what city immediately became Utah's third-largest city?

**A.** West Valley City.

---

**Q.** The slogan "Where the summer sun spends the winter" was used to promote what city?

**A.** Saint George.

---

**Q.** The Barrier Canyon pictographs are in which national park?

**A.** Canyonlands.

---

**Q.** Where does Mount Timpanogos get its name?

**A.** From the Timpanogos band of Ute Indians who lived at its base.

**Q.** For what temple is Emery County's Temple Mountain named?

**A.** Manti.

———◆———

**Q.** A river and a Great Salt Lake island were named for what nineteenth-century explorer?

**A.** John C. Frémont.

———◆———

**Q.** Which Wasatch peak was named after a mountain in Greece?

**A.** Mount Olympus.

———◆———

**Q.** Into which two geographical provinces do Utah rivers flow?

**A.** The Great Basin and the Colorado River drainage system.

———◆———

**Q.** In 1869 where did the driving of the golden spike complete the transcontinental railroad?

**A.** Promontory Summit.

———◆———

**Q.** Which county seat was named for Brigham Young?

**A.** Brigham City, Box Elder County.

———◆———

**Q.** Which county in the state has the most letters in its name?

**A.** Washington.

**Q.** Which city served as Utah's territorial capital before Salt Lake City?

**A.** Fillmore (1851–1856).

———◆———

**Q.** Which two southern Utah cities are most closely associated with the pioneer Iron Mission?

**A.** Parowan and Cedar City.

———◆———

**Q.** What is the southernmost river entering the state?

**A.** San Juan.

———◆———

**Q.** Which Utah mountain range was the last in the continental United States to be discovered?

**A.** Henry Mountains.

———◆———

**Q.** Why is one of Utah's state parks called Snow Canyon?

**A.** After Erastus Snow, an early Mormon to visit the area.

———◆———

**Q.** Why is the southwestern corner of the state known as Utah's Dixie?

**A.** Attempts were made to grow cotton there during the Civil War.

———◆———

**Q.** What is the ratio of cattle to sheep in Utah?

**A.** Two to one.

**Q.** What is the southernmost national forest in Utah?

**A.** Dixie.

———◆———

**Q.** The name of which city means "big fish"?

**A.** Panguitch.

———◆———

**Q.** What in the world was Shambip?

**A.** A county (1856–62) created from part of Tooele County.

———◆———

**Q.** Which three territories received large chunks of Utah Territory in 1861?

**A.** Nevada, Colorado, and Nebraska.

———◆———

**Q.** Where are the main television transmission facilities in Utah located?

**A.** Oquirrh Mountains.

———◆———

**Q.** What are the Greater Aneth, Greater Altamont-Bluebell, and Greater Red Wash?

**A.** Oil fields.

———◆———

**Q.** What American town was the last to receive regular mail service, beginning when a road was completed there in 1939?

**A.** Boulder, Utah.

**Q.** The western terminus of Interstate 70 is at what Utah town?

**A.** Cove Fort.

---

**Q.** Which county has the highest percentage of its land in farms?

**A.** Rich.

---

**Q.** Why was Mount Mellenthin in the LaSal Mountains named for a forest ranger?

**A.** He was killed in the line of duty (Rudolph E. Mellenthin).

---

**Q.** What is the Spanish name for the Blue Mountains in San Juan County?

**A.** Abajo.

---

**Q.** For whom is the town of Abraham in Millard County named?

**A.** Abraham H. Cannon, an early settler of the area.

---

**Q.** In the late 1800s which Tooele County town had an underground department store, cafe, and hotel?

**A.** Ajax.

---

**Q.** In the 1870s English mining investors gave which area of Alta, now known for stunning wildflowers, a poetic Celtic name for England?

**A.** Albion Basin.

**Q.** What Utah County town was first known as Mountainville?

**A.** Alpine.

---

**Q.** In 1936 which Duchesne County community chose its name through a contest sponsored by high school students?

**A.** Altamont—a composite name that refers to the nearby towns of Altonah and Mount Emmons.

---

**Q.** How many Utah farms contain more than one thousand acres?

**A.** More than thirteen hundred.

---

**Q.** Which Piute County ghost town was named for a mineral produced by its mines?

**A.** Alunite.

---

**Q.** Which two towns trace their names to the 1776 expedition led by Franciscan fathers into Utah?

**A.** Escalante and Spanish Fork.

---

**Q.** The names of two of its early female settlers were combined to form the name of which Sevier County town?

**A.** Annabella (for Ann S. Roberts and Isabella Dalton).

---

**Q.** Two mining towns built by the Utah Copper Company were named for what U.S. presidents?

**A.** Garfield (James A.) and Arthur (Chester A.).

**Q.** What valley and creek in Uintah County were named for an early fur trader in the area?

**A.** Ashley (William H.).

———◆———

**Q.** What location was the source of natural material used to pave Vernal's main street?

**A.** Asphalt Ridge.

———◆———

**Q.** Which Weber County mountain was named for a mountain in Scotland?

**A.** Ben Lomond.

———◆———

**Q.** For whom was Bingham Canyon named?

**A.** Sanford and Thomas Bingham, who ran cattle in the canyon.

———◆———

**Q.** For what was Black Dragon Canyon near Green River named?

**A.** An Indian pictograph that resembles a dragon.

———◆———

**Q.** Local residents call the Aquarius Plateau by what name?

**A.** Boulder Mountain.

———◆———

**Q.** Often the subject of environmental controversy, what trail in southern Utah was named for a rancher born on a ship sailing from Scotland to America?

**A.** Burr Trail.

**Q.** For whom was the city of Logan named?

**A.** Ephraim Logan (a fur trapper).

———◆———

**Q.** Which Wayne County settlement was named for a territorial delegate to Congress?

**A.** Caineville (John T. Caine).

———◆———

**Q.** Which western Utah town was renamed after it was said to resemble a place in Peru by the same name?

**A.** Callao.

———◆———

**Q.** Camp Floyd was named for what U.S. cabinet member under James Buchanan?

**A.** John B. Floyd, secretary of war.

———◆———

**Q.** Fort Douglas was named for what orator and political leader?

**A.** Stephen A. Douglas.

———◆———

**Q.** Which southern Utah town was jokingly referred to as "Gunshot"?

**A.** Cannonville (the town was too small to be called a cannon).

———◆———

**Q.** Which Cache County mountain range is one of the steepest in the United States?

**A.** Wellsville Mountains.

**Q.** The Carter Road across the Uinta Mountains connected which two military installations?

**A.** Fort Bridger, Wyoming, and Fort Thornburg, Utah.

---

**Q.** Which small Sanpete community is considered the closest to the geographic center of Utah?

**A.** Chester.

---

**Q.** What was the original source of water for Salt Lake City?

**A.** City Creek.

---

**Q.** In 1911 which Sanpete County community was founded as a home for Jewish settlers?

**A.** Clarion.

---

**Q.** Which Emery County town was named for a U.S. president?

**A.** Cleveland (Grover Cleveland).

---

**Q.** The river called the Fremont above Hanksville goes by what name below Hanksville?

**A.** Dirty Devil.

---

**Q.** What was the first north-south automobile route called before it was designated U.S. Highway 91?

**A.** Arrowhead Highway.

**Q.** Which south Salt Lake Valley town was named for its first Mormon bishop?

**A.** Draper (William Draper).

---

**Q.** Which Wasatch Mountain is said to resemble a desert animal?

**A.** Dromedary Peak.

---

**Q.** For whom was E. T. City (called Lake Point since 1923) at the south end of the Great Salt Lake named?

**A.** Ezra T. Benson (an early miller and Mormon apostle).

---

**Q.** What was the Colorado River above its confluence with the Green River originally called?

**A.** Grand River.

---

**Q.** The western Salt Lake County community of Magna was first called by what name?

**A.** Coonville (for Abraham Coon, who settled the area in 1854).

---

**Q.** In the 1920s, the Utah Copper Company built what town to provide housing for employees and to demonstrate the use of copper products?

**A.** Copperton.

---

**Q.** Which city, incorporated in the 1870s, was known as "the burg on the Bear"?

**A.** Corinne.

**Q.** Which Cache Valley community was named for a turn-of-the-century Union Pacific Railroad vice president?

**A.** Cornish (William Cornish).

———◆———

**Q.** Which town on the Weber River was named for the English community from which most of its settlers came?

**A.** Croydon.

———◆———

**Q.** Which county is named for the first surveyor general of Utah?

**A.** Daggett (Ellsworth Daggett).

———◆———

**Q.** Though spelled incorrectly, what 11,307-foot formation in Iron County was named for its resemblance to the profile of "the Great Commoner," a favorite of Utahns?

**A.** Brian Head (for William Jennings Bryan).

———◆———

**Q.** Which county was named for a Mormon Battalion captain, who died four months before the county was organized on June 1, 1850?

**A.** Davis (Daniel E.).

———◆———

**Q.** A tragedy is memorialized in the name of which state park?

**A.** Dead Horse Point.

———◆———

**Q.** Which Sevier County town, first known as "Little Denmark," was later renamed for a city in Denmark?

**A.** Elsinore.

**Q.** What is the only county named for a Utah territorial governor?

**A.** Emery (George W. Emery).

———◆———

**Q.** Which Salt Lake area peak was the location of a pioneer flag-raising ceremony in 1847?

**A.** Ensign Peak.

———◆———

**Q.** The names of what three Sanpete Valley communities suggest their beautiful locations?

**A.** Fountain Green, Mount Pleasant, and Fairview.

———◆———

**Q.** Which pony express trail station, named for a rider, also recalls the German author Goethe?

**A.** Faust (H. J. Faust).

———◆———

**Q.** Which Sanpete Valley town is named for the place where the Church of Jesus Christ of Latter-day Saints was organized in 1830?

**A.** Fayette (for Fayette, Seneca County, New York).

———◆———

**Q.** Which Castle Valley canyon and town were named for an early surveyor who let his men dunk him in the creek that also bears his name?

**A.** Ferron (A. D. Ferron).

———◆———

**Q.** The sun's reflections off the red rocks inspired John Wesley Powell and his men to name what area along the Green River?

**A.** Flaming Gorge.

**Q.** In 1845 Miles Goodyear built what fort on the Weber River?

**A.** Fort Buenaventura.

---

**Q.** Which Utah fort was named for a Union officer killed during the Civil War at the battle of Bull Run?

**A.** Fort Cameron, near Beaver (Col. James L. Cameron).

---

**Q.** The original Uintah Reservation was created by which U.S. president?

**A.** Abraham Lincoln (in 1861).

---

**Q.** Which Tooele County boomtown flirted briefly with the idea of taking the county seat away from Tooele City?

**A.** Mercur.

---

**Q.** Which two forts built in eastern Utah during the fur trade era were named for American frontier heroes?

**A.** Fort Davy Crockett and Fort Kit Carson.

---

**Q.** Members of which ethnic group settled the remote Tooele County town of Iosepa in the early twentieth century?

**A.** Hawaiian-Polynesian.

---

**Q.** Which central Utah community is named for the murdered leader of an 1853 railroad survey expedition?

**A.** Gunnison (Capt. John W. Gunnison).

**Q.** For whom was Heber City named?

**A.** Heber C. Kimball (counselor and friend to Brigham Young).

---

**Q.** What six rivers are also the names of counties through which they flow?

**A.** Duchesne, Grand, San Juan, Sevier, Uintah, and Weber.

---

**Q.** Which county was named for "the friend of the Mormons"?

**A.** Kane County (Thomas L. Kane).

---

**Q.** Utah's highest peak was named for what early director of the U.S. Geological Survey?

**A.** Clarence King (Kings Peak).

---

**Q.** For whom was the city of Layton named?

**A.** Christopher Layton (an early settler).

---

**Q.** Utah has how many canyons named Long Canyon?

**A.** At least twelve.

---

**Q.** What town was named for a victorious battle in the Spanish-American War?

**A.** Manila (battle of Manila Bay).

**Q.** Which mining area was named by Bavarian-born prospector Arie Pinedo for an element he found there?

**A.** Mercur (the German word for mercury).

———◆———

**Q.** Which mountains were first called "the Unknown Mountains"?

**A.** Henry.

———◆———

**Q.** Which town along the San Juan River is named for a rock formation shaped like an item of apparel?

**A.** Mexican Hat.

———◆———

**Q.** Utah's twelfth territorial governor is remembered by the name of which Salt Lake Valley city?

**A.** Murray (Eli H. Murray).

———◆———

**Q.** What happened to a woman picked up and carried about thirty feet by a tornado in Annabella in April 1970?

**A.** Remarkably, she suffered only minor injuries and a headache.

———◆———

**Q.** What town traces its name to a nineteenth-century Mormon experiment in communal living?

**A.** Orderville (United Order).

———◆———

**Q.** When it was created in 1850, the Utah Territory included what area?

**A.** All of present-day Utah, Nevada, and parts of Idaho, Wyoming, and Colorado.

**Q.** What huge limestone monolith in the House Range is the dominant landmark west of Delta?

**A.** Notch Peak.

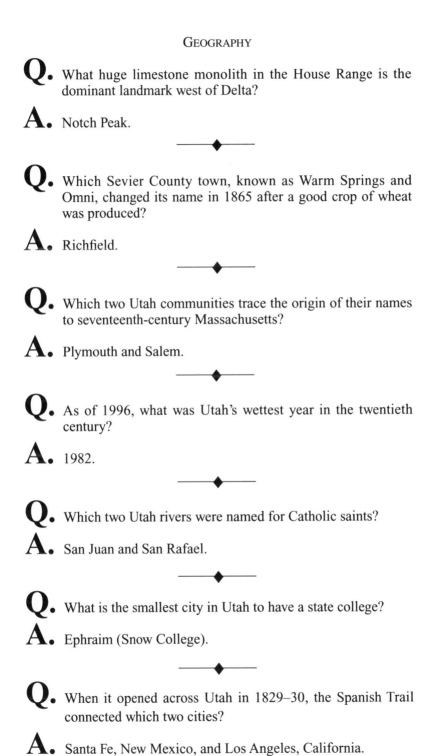

**Q.** Which Sevier County town, known as Warm Springs and Omni, changed its name in 1865 after a good crop of wheat was produced?

**A.** Richfield.

**Q.** Which two Utah communities trace the origin of their names to seventeenth-century Massachusetts?

**A.** Plymouth and Salem.

**Q.** As of 1996, what was Utah's wettest year in the twentieth century?

**A.** 1982.

**Q.** Which two Utah rivers were named for Catholic saints?

**A.** San Juan and San Rafael.

**Q.** What is the smallest city in Utah to have a state college?

**A.** Ephraim (Snow College).

**Q.** When it opened across Utah in 1829–30, the Spanish Trail connected which two cities?

**A.** Santa Fe, New Mexico, and Los Angeles, California.

**Q.** Which border town has the same name in Utah as in the adjoining state of Nevada?

**A.** Wendover.

---

**Q.** Where in Utah did the U.S. Navy place a supply depot during World War II?

**A.** Clearfield.

---

**Q.** What area crossed by the pony express during 1860–61 did not receive electricity until 1972 and private telephones until 1986?

**A.** Deep Creek, in western Utah.

---

**Q.** What was the largest quartermaster depot in the United States during World War II?

**A.** Utah General Depot (later known as Defense Depot Ogden).

---

**Q.** Approximately how often does it storm during the April Conference of the LDS Church ("Conference weather")?

**A.** Almost 70 percent of the time.

---

**Q.** Where in Utah did the U.S. Army stockpile a large number of chemical weapons?

**A.** Tooele Ordnance Depot.

---

**Q.** During World War II, what was Utah's third largest "city"?

**A.** Kearns Air Base.

**Q.** What city was known for a time as "City of Roses"?

**A.** Farmington.

———◆———

**Q.** How much of Utah's land is owned by the federal government?

**A.** 67 percent.

———◆———

**Q.** Where can one find the Aspen Giants Scenic Area, with some of the largest known quaking aspens?

**A.** Sanpete County, east of Mayfield.

———◆———

**Q.** Which county is on the north slope of the Uinta Mountains?

**A.** Daggett.

———◆———

**Q.** Under which federal act was most of Duchesne County settled?

**A.** Homestead Act.

———◆———

**Q.** How much of Utah's land is included in Indian reservations?

**A.** 4 percent.

———◆———

**Q.** Which county gave up land to create Carbon County in 1894?

**A.** Emery.

**Q.** In which county is Panguitch Lake, one of the state's prime fishing waters?

**A.** Garfield.

———◆———

**Q.** Which Juab County towns were called Salt Creek and Chicken Creek by early settlers?

**A.** Nephi and Mona.

———◆———

**Q.** How much of Utah's land is privately owned?

**A.** 22 percent.

———◆———

**Q.** During World War II what temporary "city" had the largest population (8,700) in Millard County?

**A.** Topaz (internment camp for Japanese Americans).

———◆———

**Q.** Where is a major Portland cement factory located?

**A.** Devil's Slide, Morgan County.

———◆———

**Q.** Where were the Ohio and Gold Mountain mining districts and the boomtowns of Kimberly and Bullion located?

**A.** Piute County's Tushar Mountains.

———◆———

**Q.** How much of Utah's land is owned by the state?

**A.** 7 percent.

**Q.** Where are the two Goshute Indian Reservations in Utah?

**A.** Skull Valley and the Deep Creek Mountains near the Utah-Nevada border.

———◆———

**Q.** In 1850 which nine states had part of their areas included in the proposed state of Deseret?

**A.** Utah, Idaho, Oregon, Nevada, California, Arizona, New Mexico, Colorado, and Wyoming.

———◆———

**Q.** Between which two towns is the longest stretch of interstate in the country without services?

**A.** Salina to Green River (105 miles).

———◆———

**Q.** By what name did the Shoshone Indians call the Green River?

**A.** *Seeds-kee-dee-Agie.*

———◆———

**Q.** What is the highest peak in the Henry Mountains?

**A.** Mount Ellen (11,506 feet).

———◆———

**Q.** Where is the Trappist monastery Abbey of Our Lady of the Trinity?

**A.** Huntsville.

———◆———

**Q.** Who was the leader of the Pahvant Utes for whom a Millard County town is named?

**A.** Chief Kanosh.

**Q.** What is the highest peak in the Oquirrh Mountains?

**A.** Lewiston (10,676 feet).

———◆———

**Q.** North Salt Lake is in which county?

**A.** Davis.

———◆———

**Q.** For whom was the city of Orem named?

**A.** Walter Orem (owner of an interurban railroad that ran between Salt Lake City and Provo).

———◆———

**Q.** By 1916 one could ride an electric railroad from Preston, Idaho, on the north to which Utah community on the south?

**A.** Payson.

———◆———

**Q.** What community was first known as Pond Town?

**A.** Salem.

———◆———

**Q.** Although settlers wanted to name their town in southern Utah County for the Ute chief Guffich, he declined the honor in favor of which of his sons?

**A.** Santaquin.

———◆———

**Q.** Why did the town of Tremont change its name to Tremonton?

**A.** Postal authorities confused it with Fremont, Utah.

**Q.** What Utah town has the same name as a famous Italian city?

**A.** Naples.

---

**Q.** What is the northernmost wilderness area in Utah?

**A.** Mount Naomi Wilderness Area, Cache County.

---

**Q.** Utah lies in the rain shadow of which distant mountain range?

**A.** Sierra Nevada.

---

**Q.** The Dirty Devil is a tributary of which river?

**A.** Green.

---

**Q.** Which Utah city was first known as Brownsville?

**A.** Ogden.

---

**Q.** What was unique about a geyser that resulted from oil-drilling operations in 1936 near Green River?

**A.** It spouted *cold* water (observers reported that it erupted regularly to heights of eighty to one hundred feet).

---

**Q.** How much of Utah qualifies as true desert?

**A.** About one-third.

**Q.** Which five county seats have the same name as the county?

**A.** Beaver, Duchesne, Morgan, Salt Lake, and Tooele.

◆

**Q.** What did helicopter pilots from Hill Air Force Base see on Great Salt Lake on January 23, 1972?

**A.** Icebergs (the ice formed in less salty bays, then broke loose during a warm spell and was blown onto the lake).

◆

**Q.** In what mining area did a devastating snowslide kill thirty-six people and injure thirteen on February 17, 1926?

**A.** Bingham Canyon.

◆

**Q.** About how long does it take a storm on the West Coast to reach the Wasatch Front if the jet stream is blowing over Utah?

**A.** Twenty-four hours.

# ENTERTAINMENT

## C  H  A  P  T  E  R      T  W  O

**Q.** What popular TV series starring Della Reese is filmed in Utah?

**A.** *Touched by an Angel.*

◆

**Q.** What Hollywood actress, born in Provo in 1904, starred in such movies as *Trader Horn* and the 1932 version of *The Last of the Mohicans*?

**A.** Edwina Booth.

◆

**Q.** What Broadway lyricist with forty musicals to his credit, including *The Desert Song* and *Rose Marie,* was born in Salt Lake City in 1873?

**A.** Otto Harbach.

◆

**Q.** What city has developed an auto tour of locations where movies such as *Cheyenne Autumn* and *Indiana Jones and the Last Crusade* were filmed?

**A.** Moab.

◆

**Q.** In what year was the first known circus performance in Utah?

**A.** 1866 (Great Western Circus).

**Q.** Who is the Melvin of the movie *Melvin and Howard* who claimed Howard Hughes left him a fortune in his will?

**A.** Melvin Dumar.

---

**Q.** In what year did the FCC grant KSL an FM radio permit?

**A.** 1945.

---

**Q.** On what campus is the Val A. Browning Center for the Performing Arts?

**A.** Weber State University.

---

**Q.** On what lake did the S.S. *Sho-Boat* take groups on cruises that included entertainment and dinner?

**A.** Utah Lake.

---

**Q.** The words to what song—frequently performed at Mormon funerals and on special occasions around the world—were written by Naomi Randall of North Ogden in 1957?

**A.** "I Am a Child of God."

---

**Q.** What is the present name of the popular summer event founded in 1972 as The West: America's Odyssey at Utah State University?

**A.** Festival of the American West.

---

**Q.** In 1889 what portion of Lehi's budget did the owner of the popular Lehi Opera House complain that his taxes supplied?

**A.** 50 percent.

**Q.** What red-haired star who played opposite Bing Crosby in *A Connecticut Yankee in King Arthur's Court* spent part of her childhood in Salt Lake City and often returned to visit relatives?

**A.** Rhonda Fleming.

---

**Q.** For what entertainment facility in North Salt Lake, now an LDS Church stake center, did TV star Art Linkletter help break ground in 1964?

**A.** Valley Music Hall.

---

**Q.** What did Alene Dalton, who hosted a popular children's radio program on KNAK, call herself?

**A.** The Story Princess.

---

**Q.** What Utahn wrote the words for such songs as "When It's Springtime in the Rockies"?

**A.** Maryhale Woolsey.

---

**Q.** What colorful mayor of Ogden re-energized and brought national attention to the city's Pioneer Days celebration?

**A.** Harmon W. Peery.

---

**Q.** What Utah County band was organized in part to promote the political cause of bimetallism?

**A.** Lehi Silver Band.

---

**Q.** Before it closed, where was the Hollywood Stuntmen's Hall of Fame?

**A.** Moab.

**Q.** What sad news from Utah was sent to President Ronald Reagan on May 3, 1982?

**A.** Sinbad the Sailor, the horse he rode in the TV series *Death Valley Days,* had been killed by lightning near Kanab.

---

**Q.** What was the stage name of singer James Haun, who was compared by his fans to Mario Lanza and even Caruso?

**A.** Rouvaun.

---

**Q.** The Pickleville Playhouse, a summer theater, is near which recreational area?

**A.** Bear Lake.

---

**Q.** What Utahn directed the Oscar-winning documentary *The Great American Cowboy?*

**A.** Kieth Merrill.

---

**Q.** In which Welsh festival of music and poetry did Utahns enthusiastically participate, both locally and nationally?

**A.** Eisteddfod.

---

**Q.** What conductor, violinist, and impresario produced numerous USO shows for U.S. troops in three wars?

**A.** Eugene Jelesnik.

---

**Q.** For what Utah radio stations did flamboyant disc jockey "Skinny" Johnny Mitchell work?

**A.** KNAK, KCPX, KPRQ, KSOP.

**Q.** In which *Billboard* top tunes category did Diane Duvall reach the top in December 1954 with her song "Please Don't Divorce Me"?

**A.** Hillbilly (Country).

---

**Q.** What packaged food product used in salads and desserts is so popular in Utah that it has been satirized by local playwrights, comedians, and cartoonists?

**A.** Jell-O.

---

**Q.** What outspoken star of a popular TV sitcom, which is named after her, grew up in Salt Lake City?

**A.** Roseanne (Barr).

---

**Q.** What Logan-born actor became a famous Hollywood leading man of the silent film era?

**A.** John Gilbert.

---

**Q.** With which winter-summer resort is Robert Redford associated?

**A.** Sundance.

---

**Q.** Newsmen from what "enemy" country composed a song in honor of their stay in Salt Lake City in 1955?

**A.** Soviet Union.

---

**Q.** Spotlights illuminate the canyon walls of what narrated trip up the Colorado River?

**A.** Canyonlands by Night.

**Q.** Leamarado Day in Leamington began as a celebration of the end of which war?

**A.** World War II.

**Q.** In what year did classical music station KBYU-FM begin receiving programs via satellite?

**A.** 1979.

**Q.** What Salt Lake City native starred in many movies and also hosted her own dramatic series on TV in which she always made a sweeping entrance?

**A.** Loretta Young.

**Q.** What Salt Lake City barbershop quartet won first place in an international competition in 1960?

**A.** Evans Brothers.

**Q.** Which southern Utah town was called "Little Hollywood" because so many movies were filmed there?

**A.** Kanab.

**Q.** The theater curtain in what Emery County town featured a monumental painting of the chariot race in *Ben-Hur*?

**A.** Orangeville.

**Q.** Born in Roosevelt, Utah, in 1920, what Hollywood actress was once married to baseball's Leo Durocher?

**A.** Laraine Day.

**Q.** When did KUED, channel 7, begin broadcasting?

**A.** 1958.

———◆———

**Q.** Other than Midway, what town celebrates Swiss Days?

**A.** Santa Clara.

———◆———

**Q.** With her husband, Jim, which popular folksinger of the 1950s and 1960s supervised a folklore and guitar program at the University of Utah?

**A.** Rosalie Sorrels.

———◆———

**Q.** In 1937 which station opened its Radio Playhouse with 350 seats so audiences could see live programs?

**A.** KDYL.

———◆———

**Q.** What Ogden, Utah, family of six brothers and one sister achieved international fame as musical entertainers?

**A.** The Osmonds.

———◆———

**Q.** What was the original name of the restored Ellen Eccles Theater in Logan?

**A.** Capitol Theater.

———◆———

**Q.** Park City hosts what international independent film festival each January?

**A.** Sundance Film Festival.

**Q.** Ogden auto dealer Robert H. Hinckley cofounded what communications network?

**A.** American Broadcasting Corporation.

---◆---

**Q.** In which northern Utah town did Broadway, radio, and TV actress Leora Thatcher grow up?

**A.** Logan.

---◆---

**Q.** In *This Is Cinerama,* the Mormon Tabernacle Choir sang what song as background music?

**A.** "America the Beautiful."

---◆---

**Q.** In 1980, KWHO began broadcasting a two-hour Saturday morning program in what language?

**A.** Spanish.

---◆---

**Q.** Which Utah national park is shown in the opening sequence of *Indiana Jones and the Last Crusade?*

**A.** Arches.

---◆---

**Q.** What 1943 boy-with-a-horse movie starring Roddy McDowell was filmed in Utah?

**A.** *My Friend Flicka.*

---◆---

**Q.** In 1922 Utah-born dancer Winifred Kimball Shaughnessy, later known as Natacha Rambova, married what silent film idol?

**A.** Rudolph Valentino.

**Q.** What future U.S. senator emceed for the KSL Players on radio?

**A.** Wallace F. Bennett.

———◆———

**Q.** For which two stars of the 1944 movie *Buffalo Bill* did Mrs. Della Pugh of Kanab act as a stand-in?

**A.** Maureen O'Hara and Linda Darnell.

———◆———

**Q.** An appropriation to set up an educational TV station was vetoed by which governor?

**A.** J. Bracken Lee.

———◆———

**Q.** What role did Utah actor Moroni Olsen play in the 1944 film *Ali Baba and the Forty Thieves*?

**A.** Caliph of Baghdad.

———◆———

**Q.** What was the title of the 1947 "Utah centennial movie" denounced in the state senate as a "fourth-class, trashy picture"?

**A.** *Ramrod.*

———◆———

**Q.** What 1944 Deanna Durbin movie featured forty covered wagons in a scene shot near Navajo Lake?

**A.** *Can't Help Singing.*

———◆———

**Q.** What horrifying incident in Sandy history was depicted in the 1992 CBS-TV movie *Deliver Them from Evil*?

**A.** The siege of Alta View Hospital by Richard Worthington in 1991.

**Q.** What National Broadcast Foundation award did KSL Radio receive in 1974 for its pioneering work?

**A.** Golden Mike Award.

---

**Q.** Where did Twentieth Century-Fox shoot its 1939 epic *Drums Along the Mohawk* because of land contours similar to New York's Mohawk Valley and the resemblance of quaking aspen to birch?

**A.** Near Cedar Breaks National Monument.

---

**Q.** What historical character did Utah Jazz superstar Karl Malone portray in a 1993 movie based on the life of Porter Rockwell?

**A.** Elijah Abel.

---

**Q.** Members of which Indian tribe officially petitioned a Hollywood studio in 1946 for more work in the movies?

**A.** Navajo.

---

**Q.** What kind of music did KUER, now a classics, news, and jazz station, also play in the 1960s when students were involved in broadcasting?

**A.** Rock 'n' roll.

---

**Q.** What actor played the title role in the 1940 movie *Brigham Young—Frontiersman*?

**A.** Dean Jagger.

---

**Q.** What was the hometown of silent film actress Betty Compson?

**A.** Beaver.

**Q.** When it opened on January 6, 1907, the Alpine Amusement Hall was equipped for what activity other than dramatic productions and dancing?

**A.** Basketball.

———◆———

**Q.** What Utah boxer had to learn Hollywood-style fighting for his film debut as a bartender in *Devil's Brigade*?

**A.** Gene Fullmer.

———◆———

**Q.** What did radio station KUTA begin reading to children on Sunday mornings in 1945?

**A.** Sunday "funnies" (comic strips).

———◆———

**Q.** In 1965 what Oscar-winning African-American star was thrown from a horse during a battle scene being filmed near Kanab for the movie *Duel at Diablo*?

**A.** Sidney Poitier.

———◆———

**Q.** Over what body of water was the Japanese attack on Wake Island re-created for the 1942 movie *Wake Island*?

**A.** Great Salt Lake.

———◆———

**Q.** In what 1963 biblical epic did Utah national guardsmen portray Roman soldiers?

**A.** *The Greatest Story Ever Told.*

———◆———

**Q.** What Utah studio produced the *Grizzly Adams* TV series?

**A.** Sunn Classics, Park City.

**Q.** Which Disney movie starring Vera Miles received the BYU Family Movie Award in 1967?

**A.** *Follow Me, Boys.*

---

**Q.** What Ogden native was the first Utahn to become a successful Hollywood director and producer in the 1920s and 1930s?

**A.** James Cruze.

---

**Q.** What actress from Richmond appeared as a bathing beauty in Mack Sennett films?

**A.** Mary Thurman.

---

**Q.** Organized in 1917, what Utah film company produced *The Lust of the Ages* as its first drama?

**A.** Ogden Pictures Corporation.

---

**Q.** Which Salt Lake City mayor was a pioneering figure in radio broadcasting?

**A.** Earl J. Glade.

---

**Q.** What birth disorder was the subject of the 1980 Oscar-winning short film *Board and Care,* filmed by KUED cinematographer Paul Cheesman?

**A.** Down's syndrome.

---

**Q.** Where was the 1943 Technicolor epic *Arabian Nights* filmed?

**A.** Coral Pink Sand Dunes.

**Q.** Where were many outdoor scenes for *Gunsmoke, Death Valley Days,* and *Wagon Train* filmed?

**A.** The set of a western town erected in Johnson Canyon near Kanab.

━━━◆━━━

**Q.** Col. Paul Tibbetts, the pilot of the plane that dropped the first atomic bomb, was portrayed by what actor in *Above and Beyond* (1952), which was partly filmed in Wendover?

**A.** Robert Taylor.

━━━◆━━━

**Q.** Which Utah singing sisters developed a popular following on radio and had recorded over one hundred songs by 1943?

**A.** King Sisters.

━━━◆━━━

**Q.** Where will you find thousands of Salt Lakers eating lunch the Friday after Labor Day?

**A.** At the Greek Festival.

━━━◆━━━

**Q.** What was the title of the 1980 romantic fantasy based on the life of Utah actress Maude Adams, starring Jane Seymour and Christopher Reeve?

**A.** *Somewhere in Time.*

━━━◆━━━

**Q.** What was the first drive-in movie theater in the Mountain West?

**A.** Park Vu Drive-In, 3821 South 100 East, Salt Lake City.

━━━◆━━━

**Q.** What 1969 Robert Redford movie was filmed in part at the actor's Sundance resort?

**A.** *Downhill Racer.*

**Q.** What actor from Ogden appeared in *Bataan, Madame Curie,* and *See Here, Private Hargrove?*

**A.** Robert Walker.

---

**Q.** What was the title of the 1979 documentary film, which won a Rocky Mountain regional Oscar, about an illegal alien living in Provo?

**A.** *Wetback.*

---

**Q.** When did the first regularly scheduled telecast in the intermountain area go on the air?

**A.** April 19, 1948.

---

**Q.** What actor described southeastern Utah as "where God put the West"?

**A.** John Wayne.

---

**Q.** When was the Miss Riverton Pageant first organized?

**A.** 1955.

---

**Q.** Which Utah ghost town was the location for the 1969 movie *Butch Cassidy and the Sundance Kid?*

**A.** Grafton.

---

**Q.** A scene in the movie *Thelma and Louise* was filmed in what eastern Utah diner?

**A.** Silver Grill, in Thompson.

**Q.** When was the first radio broadcast made in Utah?

**A.** May 1922, by KZN.

―――――◆―――――

**Q.** What popular Utah band leader, who gave hundreds of performances between 1885 and 1936, was a contemporary of John Philip Sousa?

**A.** John Held.

―――――◆―――――

**Q.** In what year was the merry-go-round, which is still functioning, placed at the Lagoon amusement park?

**A.** 1906.

―――――◆―――――

**Q.** Why does Richmond hold its Black and White Days?

**A.** To exhibit Holstein dairy cattle.

―――――◆―――――

**Q.** In what year did the Saltair resort on the Great Salt Lake open?

**A.** 1893.

―――――◆―――――

**Q.** When did Cedar City's Shakespeare Festival begin?

**A.** 1962.

―――――◆―――――

**Q.** How many TV channels could viewers in the Salt Lake City area receive by the summer of 1954?

**A.** Three.

**Q.** In what year was the Wasatch Mountain Club organized?

**A.** 1912.

---

**Q.** What city calls itself "the Festival City"?

**A.** Cedar City.

---

**Q.** For what film did Ogden-born Hal Ashby receive an Academy Award in 1967?

**A.** *In the Heat of the Night.*

---

**Q.** For what two movies did Frank Borzage of Salt Lake City win Academy Awards for best director?

**A.** *Seventh Heaven* (1928) and *Bad Girl* (1932).

---

**Q.** In what year did Logan's first radio station, KVNU, go on the air?

**A.** 1938.

---

**Q.** Tony Geary, Emmy Award-winning actor for his role as Luke Spencer in *General Hospital,* was born in 1947 in what city?

**A.** Coalville.

---

**Q.** What Salt Lake City native composed "When You Wish upon a Star"?

**A.** Leigh Harline (1907–69).

**Q.** What semiannual church event was first televised in April 1948?

**A.** LDS Church Conference.

———◆———

**Q.** For what 1932 film based on a Hemingway novel did Charles B. Lang, born in Bluff in 1902, win an Oscar as director of photography?

**A.** *A Farewell to Arms.*

———◆———

**Q.** Where and when did Ogden-born Donny Osmond make his vocal debut at the age of four?

**A.** *The Andy Williams Show,* 1961.

———◆———

**Q.** What Salt Lake City native was cast by his friend Charlie Chaplin as Big Jim McKay in the film *The Gold Rush*?

**A.** Mark Swain.

———◆———

**Q.** What small town was the birthplace in 1922 of actress Marie Windsor, born Emily Marie Bertelson?

**A.** Marysvale.

———◆———

**Q.** What Bountiful native and University of Utah graduate won a Tony as best supporting actor on Broadway in 1971?

**A.** Keene Curtis.

———◆———

**Q.** What social problem was addressed in *The Child and the Beast,* a 1915 film based on a Salt Lake City judge's cases?

**A.** Drunkenness.

**Q.** What Salt Lake City native has performed in such movies as *The China Syndrome, Cocoon, The Electric Horseman,* and *Tender Mercies*?

**A.** Wilford Brimley.

---

**Q.** What Utahn played the lead role in the television series *Father Murphy*?

**A.** Merlin Olsen.

---

**Q.** What country singer injured her knee skiing at Park City in December 1996, the day after giving a concert in Salt Lake City?

**A.** Reba McEntire.

---

**Q.** What popular American folk song was inspired by a brightly colored hill in Marysvale Canyon?

**A.** "The Big Rock Candy Mountain."

---

**Q.** What popular pioneer social activity often took place in the bath house at Warm Springs northwest of Salt Lake City?

**A.** Dancing, including fancy balls.

---

**Q.** What musical instrument did Thomas Giles, a blind man from Wales, earn his living playing in pioneer Utah?

**A.** Harp.

---

**Q.** How much did the first musical group to present a concert tour in northern Utah (Deseret Philharmonic Society) gross in 1855?

**A.** $218.90.

**Q.** What was *Keepapitchinin*?

**A.** A humorous newspaper of the early 1870s.

———◆———

**Q.** What were early theater patrons in Salt Lake City required to check at the door?

**A.** Firearms.

———◆———

**Q.** For what use did Harry Bowring offer his unfinished home in the fall of 1859?

**A.** As a theater.

———◆———

**Q.** For which two forms of dance performance is Brigham Young University internationally recognized?

**A.** Ballroom dancing and folk dancing.

———◆———

**Q.** In what famous ballad associated with the forty-niners are Brigham Young and plural marriage satirized?

**A.** "Sweet Betsy from Pike."

———◆———

**Q.** What was a "wood dance" in rural Utah?

**A.** A community dance, often including supper, following a day of gathering and chopping wood.

———◆———

**Q.** In the Utah Territory, Domenico Ballo was known for what two skills?

**A.** Band leading and music teaching.

**Q.** When pioneer parents failed to heed "Children in arms not admitted," how did managers of the Salt Lake Theatre reword the notice?

**A.** "Babies in arms ten dollars extra."

◆

**Q.** What popular Gilbert and Sullivan operetta was first performed in Utah in April 1879?

**A.** *H.M.S. Pinafore.*

◆

**Q.** What instrument was first played in Utah by William C. Dunbar in 1859?

**A.** Bagpipes.

◆

**Q.** What group won the first American College Dance Festival competition in 1981?

**A.** University of Utah's Performing Dance Company.

◆

**Q.** In 1911 what anti-Mormon film produced in Denmark did Governor Spry attempt to censor?

**A.** *A Victim of the Mormons.*

◆

**Q.** What did a prominent woman at an early theater performance in Salt Lake City proudly pass around between acts for the audience to inspect?

**A.** The first set of false teeth in the city.

◆

**Q.** What Salt Lake City building erected in 1852 was used for such activities as dances, concerts, plays, and choir rehearsals?

**A.** Social Hall.

**Q.** Pioneer leaders disapproved of what type of dance?

**A.** Waltz (couple dancing).

◆

**Q.** Tuacahn, the arts facility where the outdoor musical epic *Utah!* is performed, is in what small town?

**A.** Ivins.

◆

**Q.** Which town includes a snow sculpture competition as part of its annual Winter Fest?

**A.** Park City.

◆

**Q.** What town hosts the World Folkfest each summer?

**A.** Springville.

◆

**Q.** What is the state song?

**A.** "Utah, We Love Thee."

◆

**Q.** In which theater were audiences shocked during an 1869 performance of *Oliver Twist* when actress Lucille Western, as Nancy, appeared with a thin slice of raw beef on her cheek to simulate bruised, broken skin?

**A.** Salt Lake Theatre.

◆

**Q.** How did people in small towns pay for theater and dance admissions in the nineteenth century?

**A.** With vegetables and other farm products.

**Q.** In which two Utah cities do Egyptian Theaters reflect the craze for Egyptian Revival architecture inspired by the discovery of King Tut's tomb in 1922?

**A.** Ogden and Park City.

---

**Q.** Especially known for her portrayal of Peter Pan, who was the first Utah-born actress to achieve fame on Broadway?

**A.** Maude Adams.

---

**Q.** As a young man, which Utah governor appeared in many local plays, often as the romantic lead?

**A.** Heber M. Wells.

---

**Q.** What building of the early 1860s was known as "the Cathedral in the Desert"?

**A.** Salt Lake Theatre.

---

**Q.** What was the first motion picture filmed on location in Utah?

**A.** *Deadwood Dick* (1922).

---

**Q.** When was Pioneer Memorial Theater at the University of Utah completed?

**A.** 1962 (the centennial year of the Salt Lake Theatre, of which it is a replica).

---

**Q.** What theater was restored by Salt Lake County as part of the 1976 U.S. Bicentennial celebration?

**A.** Capitol Theater.

**Q.** How far is it for Salt Lakers to travel to the popular gambling-entertainment spot of Wendover, Nevada?

**A.** 120 miles.

◆

**Q.** In which former high school building is Salt Lake Community College's Grand Theater located?

**A.** South High School.

◆

**Q.** What nationally known singer of labor folk songs was a candidate for the U.S. Senate for the Peace and Freedom Party in 1968?

**A.** Bruce "Utah" Phillips.

◆

**Q.** What natural landmark along the Hole-in-the-Rock Trail got its name from its use for pioneer recreation?

**A.** Dance Hall Rock.

◆

**Q.** Where were the first theatrical performances held in Utah?

**A.** Bowery on Temple Square, in 1850.

◆

**Q.** Where does one go in August to celebrate Watermelon Days?

**A.** Green River.

◆

**Q.** Where is the Paiute Restoration Powwow held in June?

**A.** Cedar City.

**Q.** What popular musical group recorded the song "Salt Lake City" in 1965?

**A.** The Beach Boys.

———◆———

**Q.** Featuring live performances and arts and crafts, the Salt Lake City Arts Festival is held in what venue?

**A.** Triad Center.

———◆———

**Q.** What was the first type of musical group formed in most Utah towns?

**A.** Brass band.

———◆———

**Q.** What Salt Lake City family produces musicals and comedies at its theater year-round?

**A.** Hale (Hale Center Theater).

———◆———

**Q.** Who is thought to have said, "I may not walk the straight and narrow, but I try to cross it as often as I can"?

**A.** J. Golden Kimball.

———◆———

**Q.** What unique Sunday morning radio program has been hosted by Klaus Rathke?

**A.** The German Hour.

———◆———

**Q.** Where is the Timpanogos Story-Telling Festival held?

**A.** Orem.

**Q.** In what pageant is the Irrigation Ditch Dance performed?

**A.** Castle Valley.

---

**Q.** What popular Utah musical group wrote the music for the movie *Where the Red Ferns Grow*?

**A.** The Osmonds.

---

**Q.** Where is the Southern Utah Folklife Festival held?

**A.** Springdale, at the entrance to Zion National Park.

---

**Q.** For which festival are both audience and performers transported by boat on the Colorado River to a natural amphitheater?

**A.** Moab Music Festival.

---

**Q.** What is the name of the popular southeastern Utah folksong that includes the lines, "I trade at Mons's store./With bullet holes in the door./His calico treasure my horse can measure/when I'm drunk and feeling sore"?

**A.** "Blue Mountain" (by Fred J. Keller).

---

**Q.** Citing its negative depiction of pioneer life in Utah's Dixie, LDS Church leaders rebuked pioneer George A. Hicks for what song he wrote in 1865?

**A.** "Once I Lived in Cottonwood."

---

**Q.** In what building did a Mormon choir perform as part of a Catholic High Mass on May 25, 1879?

**A.** Saint George Tabernacle.

**Q.** Who sports red boots, blue jeans, a green shirt, a yellow bandanna, a white hat, and is more than fifty feet tall?

**A.** Wendover Wil (a freestanding neon sign built in 1951).

---

**Q.** What is the state's largest July Fourth celebration?

**A.** Provo's Freedom Festival.

---

**Q.** Where is the Shooting Star Saloon?

**A.** Huntsville.

---

**Q.** The Mountain Man Rendezvous takes place in what state park?

**A.** Fort Buenaventura, in Ogden.

---

**Q.** What cult film classic did Hal Ashby direct in 1972?

**A.** *Harold and Maude.*

---

**Q.** What was the name of the movie palace that opened on Main Street in Salt Lake City in 1913, claiming to be the largest in the world?

**A.** American Theatre.

---

**Q.** What institution is housed in the old Wasatch Plunge swimming facility in Salt Lake City?

**A.** Children's Museum of Utah.

# HISTORY

**Q.** What issue generated the most controversy at the 1895 Constitutional Convention?

**A.** Woman suffrage.

———◆———

**Q.** What forger of historic documents is serving a prison sentence for two murders?

**A.** Mark Hofmann.

———◆———

**Q.** In 1972 which Democrat was elected governor for an unprecedented third term?

**A.** Calvin L. Rampton.

———◆———

**Q.** Female descendants of those who came to Utah before 1869 founded what organization in 1901?

**A.** Daughters of Utah Pioneers.

———◆———

**Q.** Which president signed the Utah Statehood Proclamation on January 4, 1896?

**A.** Grover Cleveland.

**Q.** Who were the three African-American members of the first Mormon pioneer group?

**A.** Green Flake, Hark Lay, and Oscar Crosby.

———◆———

**Q.** Who was the first American to travel the length of Utah from north to south?

**A.** Jedediah Smith.

———◆———

**Q.** Most Mormons belonged to what political organization before the Republican and Democratic Parties were organized in Utah?

**A.** People's Party.

———◆———

**Q.** Lead extracted from the Lincoln Mine in Beaver County, opened in 1858 as one of the first mines in Utah, was used for what purpose after shipment to Salt Lake City?

**A.** To make ammunition.

———◆———

**Q.** What territorial governor, leaving his post in Utah after less than a month, was attacked and beaten in Parley's Canyon in 1861?

**A.** John W. Dawson.

———◆———

**Q.** What organization did U.S. senator Thomas Kearns blame for his failure to win reelection in 1905?

**A.** Mormon Church.

———◆———

**Q.** In 1918 from what country did sixty families come to work in the sugar beet fields and establish a colony near Garland, Box Elder County?

**A.** Mexico.

**Q.** How many people were in the first group of Mormons, called the Pioneer Company, that set out for Utah?

**A.** 148 (143 men, 3 women, 2 children).

———◆———

**Q.** Eurithe K. LaBarthe of Salt Lake City and Sarah E. Anderson of Ogden achieved what distinction in 1896?

**A.** First women elected to the Utah House of Representatives.

———◆———

**Q.** What two Franciscan priests led the first exploratory expedition to Utah in 1776?

**A.** Francisco Atanasio Dominguez and Silvestre Velez de Escalante.

———◆———

**Q.** In what year was Southern Utah University founded as the Branch Normal School?

**A.** 1897.

———◆———

**Q.** What church founded Salt Lake City's Westminster College?

**A.** Presbyterian.

———◆———

**Q.** What was the first overland emigrant group to pass through the present state of Utah?

**A.** Bartleson-Bidwell party (en route to California in 1841).

———◆———

**Q.** What is Utah's nickname?

**A.** Beehive State.

**Q.** On what date was the golden spike driven, linking the Pacific and the Atlantic coasts by rail?

**A.** May 10, 1869.

———◆———

**Q.** How many husbands did Utah's Silver Queen have?

**A.** Four.

———◆———

**Q.** In what year did the territorial legislature grant women in Utah the right to vote?

**A.** 1870.

———◆———

**Q.** What was the University of Utah called from 1850 to 1894?

**A.** University of Deseret.

———◆———

**Q.** Since statehood, how many Utah governors have been born outside of the United States?

**A.** Three (John C. Cutler and William Spry, England; Simon Bamberger, Germany).

———◆———

**Q.** What Utahn served as secretary of agriculture under President Eisenhower?

**A.** Ezra Taft Benson.

———◆———

**Q.** Who was Utah Territory's first delegate to Congress?

**A.** John M. Bernhisel.

**Q.** The conflict between the Mormons and the Utes fought during 1865–68 is known by what name?

**A.** Black Hawk War.

◆

**Q.** Which governor was a recognized expert in water engineering?

**A.** George D. Clyde.

◆

**Q.** What is the oldest non-Mormon church building in Utah?

**A.** Corinne Methodist Church (1870).

◆

**Q.** On July 22, 1847, which two men were the first Mormons to enter the Great Salt Lake Valley?

**A.** Orson Pratt and Erastus Snow.

◆

**Q.** Which governor promoted the first important civil rights legislation in Utah?

**A.** Calvin L. Rampton (1965–1977).

◆

**Q.** What did law officers do to the three men who allegedly attacked territorial governor John W. Dawson?

**A.** Shot and killed them.

◆

**Q.** The state legislature cast the thirty-sixth and deciding vote to ratify what amendment to the U.S. Constitution?

**A.** Twenty-first, repealing Prohibition (1933).

**Q.** What did Charles A. Steen call the uranium bonanza he discovered in 1952?

**A.** Mi Vida Mine.

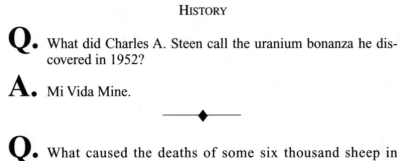

**Q.** What caused the deaths of some six thousand sheep in Tooele County in 1968?

**A.** Testing of chemical weapons at Dugway Proving Ground.

**Q.** What was the Wooden Gun Rebellion of November 1870?

**A.** Illegal drill by the Nauvoo Legion.

**Q.** Who licensed Antoine Robidoux to operate a trading post in the Uinta Basin in 1831?

**A.** The Mexican government.

**Q.** What did Governors Herbert B. Maw and J. Bracken Lee have in common?

**A.** They lost bids for reelection to third terms.

**Q.** What is a *fourno*, once common in Italian immigrant neighborhoods in Carbon County?

**A.** Outdoor baking oven.

**Q.** What was the first large factory in Utah?

**A.** Provo Woolen Mills.

**Q.** Where were more than five hundred captured German seamen sent as prisoners of war in 1917?

**A.** Fort Douglas.

———◆———

**Q.** What two Canadian-born entrepreneurs were partners in the Silver King Mine, purchased the *Salt Lake Tribune* together, and built mansions near each other on South Temple Street in Salt Lake City?

**A.** David Keith and Thomas Kearns.

———◆———

**Q.** The U.S. Customs Service gave Salt Lake City what designation in 1969?

**A.** Port of entry.

———◆———

**Q.** Leaving Sacramento on April 3, 1860, the first Pony Express rider arrived in Salt Lake City on what date?

**A.** April 7, 1860.

———◆———

**Q.** What precious metal was discovered in 1864 in the present ski resort of Alta?

**A.** Silver.

———◆———

**Q.** What Utah governor joked that he was both a "Pa" and a "Ma"?

**A.** Herbert B. Maw.

———◆———

**Q.** What did the Eastern Utah Railway and Summit County Railway have in common?

**A.** Both reached Park City from Coalville along parallel routes in 1880.

**Q.** What controversial facility opened in December 1908 as a direct result of Salt Lake police and city officials' actions?

**A.** A brothel.

◆

**Q.** Governor Simon Bamberger is known for what three "firsts"?

**A.** First non-Mormon, Democratic, and Jewish governor of Utah (1917).

◆

**Q.** What is Utah's oldest bank still in operation?

**A.** Zions Bank, established in 1875.

◆

**Q.** What Utahn was the first woman in America to chair a major national political party?

**A.** Democrat Jean M. Westwood (1972).

◆

**Q.** What father and son have represented Utah in the U.S. Senate?

**A.** Wallace F. Bennett (1951–75) and Robert F. Bennett (1992–).

◆

**Q.** In what two places are the state's major oil refineries located?

**A.** North Salt Lake and Woods Cross.

◆

**Q.** How many children did Brigham Young have?

**A.** Fifty-six.

**Q.** In 1899 the Reverend J. W. Washington became the first pastor of what African-American congregation?

**A.** Calvary Baptist Church, Salt Lake City.

———◆———

**Q.** As of 1997, who is Utah's longest serving U.S. senator?

**A.** Reed Smoot (1903–33).

———◆———

**Q.** In 1940 clothing factory owner Ada Williams Quinn of Ogden announced her candidacy for what public office?

**A.** Governor of Utah.

———◆———

**Q.** What railroad was completed between Salt Lake City and Denver in 1883?

**A.** Denver & Rio Grande.

———◆———

**Q.** What ethnic restaurant fare was first advertised in the 1908 Salt Lake City directory?

**A.** Mexican food (Abraham Mejia's restaurant at First South and Commercial Streets).

———◆———

**Q.** What non-Mormon building, used for church services and meetings, was erected on Third South in Salt Lake City in 1866?

**A.** Independence Hall.

———◆———

**Q.** What Ogden native is known as "the greatest firearms inventor the world has ever known"?

**A.** John Moses Browning (credited with 128 gun patents).

**Q.** What hospital was constructed to care for World War II casualties?

**A.** Bushnell General Hospital, Brigham City.

———◆———

**Q.** What Utahn was the presidential nominee of the Farmer-Labor Party in 1920?

**A.** Parley P. Christensen.

———◆———

**Q.** Major railroads constructed several branch lines in northern and central Utah in the early twentieth century to haul what commodity?

**A.** Sugar beets.

———◆———

**Q.** Who replaced Brigham Young as Utah's second territorial governor?

**A.** Alfred Cumming (1857).

———◆———

**Q.** What European country supplied more immigrants to Utah in the nineteenth century than any other except Great Britain?

**A.** Denmark.

———◆———

**Q.** Herbert S. Auerbach, heir to a merchandising fortune, translated what early Spanish document for publication by the Utah State Historical Society?

**A.** Diary (1776) of Father Escalante.

———◆———

**Q.** Before the completion of the State Capitol in 1916, what building housed state officials?

**A.** Salt Lake City and County Building.

**Q.** What political party achieved its greatest success in 1911 when it elected thirty-three city officials, including the entire administrations of five towns: Murray, Eureka, Joseph, Mammoth, and Stockton?

**A.** Socialist.

———◆———

**Q.** For what school did two Holy Cross sisters collect funds by visiting rough mining camps from Alta to Ophir in the 1870s?

**A.** Saint Mary's Academy (opened in 1875 in Salt Lake City).

———◆———

**Q.** What unusual building material was used by WPA workers to construct the hangar at the Bryce Canyon Airport in 1936?

**A.** Ponderosa pine logs.

———◆———

**Q.** Why did the Nathan Tenney family of Grafton, Washington County, name a son, born circa 1861, Marvelous Flood Tenney?

**A.** The wagon in which his mother lay awaiting delivery was almost swept away by the flooding Virgin River.

———◆———

**Q.** President Warren G. Harding appointed what Utah congressman and senator to the U.S. Supreme Court?

**A.** George Sutherland.

———◆———

**Q.** Who was the first principal, or president, of Brigham Young University?

**A.** Karl G. Maeser.

———◆———

**Q.** Who was the first U.S. Army officer to lead an expedition into Utah?

**A.** John C. Frémont (1843).

**Q.** What was the name of Utah's first territorial militia?

**A.** Nauvoo Legion.

———◆———

**Q.** Where did bomber crews, including the crew of the *Enola Gay* which dropped the atomic bomb on Hiroshima, train during World War II?

**A.** Wendover Air Base.

———◆———

**Q.** What presidential candidate received more than 80 percent of the Utah vote in 1896?

**A.** William Jennings Bryan, who lost the election.

———◆———

**Q.** Where was a parachute manufacturing plant located during World War II?

**A.** Manti.

———◆———

**Q.** The slogan "We want a Dern good governor and we don't mean Mabey" was part of what gubernatorial campaign?

**A.** When Democrat George Dern defeated incumbent Charles Mabey in 1924.

———◆———

**Q.** In which county did a group of Quakers spend a dozen years, beginning in 1893, trying to establish a farm settlement, the Swan Lake Project?

**A.** Millard.

———◆———

**Q.** During the Berlin airlift after World War II, what Garland resident was called the "Berlin Candy Bomber" for dropping candy to German children?

**A.** Gail S. Halvorsen.

**Q.** In 1846 what caused the traveler Heinrich Leinhard to experience "an almost unbearable smarting or itching over the whole body"?

**A.** Swimming in the Great Salt Lake, then dressing without washing off the salt.

———◆———

**Q.** What shelter, now part of a state park near the Nevada border, was occupied as early as 10,000 B.C.?

**A.** Danger Cave.

———◆———

**Q.** Why did Danish immigrants in Sanpete County call each other by such names as False Bottom Larsen, Alphabet Hansen, Jake Butcher, and Dan Wheelmaker Jensen?

**A.** Many people had the same names.

———◆———

**Q.** Who is thought to be the first European to set foot in Utah?

**A.** Juan Maria Antonio Rivera (1765).

———◆———

**Q.** Who was the first known African American in Utah?

**A.** James Beckwourth (a fur trader).

———◆———

**Q.** What occupation did Brigham Young encourage young unmarried women in small towns to learn in the mid-1860s?

**A.** Telegraph operating.

———◆———

**Q.** What Bingham High School graduate was named treasurer of the United States by President Eisenhower and later served as state treasurer of California?

**A.** Ivy Baker Priest.

**Q.** What country claimed ownership of the present state of Utah until the Treaty of Guadalupe Hidalgo was signed in 1848?

**A.** Mexico.

---

**Q.** What ethnic enclave in early-twentieth-century Salt Lake City centered around Plum Alley?

**A.** Chinatown.

---

**Q.** Who was the first female attorney general elected in Utah?

**A.** Jan Graham (1992).

---

**Q.** In 1848 Amos H. Neff opened what type of facility as the first of its kind in Utah?

**A.** Retail store.

---

**Q.** Which legendary champion of workers' rights visited striking Carbon County miners in 1904?

**A.** Mother Jones.

---

**Q.** What Salt Lake City woman was twice elected president of the National Council of Jewish Women?

**A.** Esther Landa.

---

**Q.** Which two Utahns were listed as billionaires in *Forbes* magazine in 1996?

**A.** Jon M. Huntsman and James L. Sorenson.

**Q.** What caused the deaths of 172 men at Castle Gate in 1924, the state's second-worst disaster?

**A.** Coal mine explosion.

———◆———

**Q.** For what offense were prominent businessmen arrested early in 1923 in a hotel dining room?

**A.** Smoking (the legislature had banned smoking in 1921).

———◆———

**Q.** Why did Utah have only one U.S. senator during 1899–1901?

**A.** The state legislature failed to elect one.

———◆———

**Q.** Who was the first U.S. president to visit Utah?

**A.** Ulysses S. Grant.

———◆———

**Q.** What Utah banker helped design FDR's New Deal and served as head of the Federal Reserve?

**A.** Marriner S. Eccles.

———◆———

**Q.** What decoration did the French government bestow on Maud Fitch of Eureka for her heroism as an ambulance driver in World War I?

**A.** Croix de Guerre.

———◆———

**Q.** From what city was Layton finally able to separate in 1902 after three decades of feuding over taxes and lack of services?

**A.** Kaysville.

**Q.** Which U.S. senator was called "the Great Protectionist" for his support of high tariffs?

**A.** Reed Smoot.

---

**Q.** Who was the first African American elected to the Utah legislature?

**A.** Reverend Robert Davis, a Democrat from Ogden (1976).

---

**Q.** What conflict is sometimes called the last Indian uprising in the United States?

**A.** The Posey War, in San Juan County (1923).

---

**Q.** When was the state sales tax introduced in Utah?

**A.** 1933, as qualification for federal funds during the Great Depression.

---

**Q.** The activities of what Mexican rebel caused Mormon colonists in Chihuahua, Mexico, to relocate to towns such as Blanding, Utah?

**A.** Pancho Villa.

---

**Q.** Where did Marie Ogden found her Home of Truth religious organization in the 1930s?

**A.** Dry Valley north of Monticello, San Juan County.

---

**Q.** What are the five major ethnic groups who comprise Utah's Polynesian population?

**A.** Tongans, Samoans, Hawaiians, Maoris, and Tahitians.

**Q.** The 1886 legislature made what crime a felony punishable by up to ten years in prison and a fine of up to five thousand dollars?

**A.** Cattle rustling.

———◆———

**Q.** What presidential candidate came in third in Utah in the 1992 election?

**A.** Bill Clinton.

———◆———

**Q.** What do the initials ZCMI stand for?

**A.** Zions Cooperative Mercantile Institution.

———◆———

**Q.** Who was the first Japanese American elected to the Salt Lake County Commission (1990)?

**A.** Randy Horiuchi.

———◆———

**Q.** What was Utah's highest unemployment rate during the Great Depression?

**A.** 35.8 percent (in 1933).

———◆———

**Q.** What immigrant group preceded the Mormon pioneers into the Salt Lake Valley by a year?

**A.** Donner party (in 1846).

———◆———

**Q.** With what development is the name John H. Koyle associated?

**A.** The Dream Mine, east of Payson.

**Q.** Who was the first governor of the state of Utah?

**A.** Heber M. Wells (1896–1905).

◆

**Q.** Whom did farmers in Salt Lake County sue in the early 1900s, claiming pollution ruined their crops?

**A.** Smelting and refining companies.

◆

**Q.** What was Utah's first federal reclamation project?

**A.** Strawberry Valley project, completed in 1922.

◆

**Q.** How many perished in 1856 when early snowstorms ravaged the Martin and Willie handcart companies?

**A.** Approximately 200 out of the 1,075 emigrants.

◆

**Q.** Born in Brown's Park in 1878, Ann Bassett is suspected by some historians as being what notorious companion of the Wild Bunch?

**A.** The outlaw queen Etta Place.

◆

**Q.** What desert town established in the late nineteenth century had attracted over two hundred Polynesian residents by 1916?

**A.** Iosepa, Tooele County.

◆

**Q.** What crime did "mountain common law" in pioneer times often treat as justifiable homicide?

**A.** One's killing a man who had seduced one's close female relative.

**Q.** Which Jewish merchant was one of the original stockholders of ZCMI?

**A.** Nicholas Ransohoff.

◆

**Q.** Investors from which European country were heavily involved in Utah mining ventures beginning in the early 1870s?

**A.** Great Britain.

◆

**Q.** What is another name for Shoshonean peoples?

**A.** Numic or Numic-speaking.

◆

**Q.** What did Kit Carson carve on Fremont Island in 1843?

**A.** A cross.

◆

**Q.** In what year was the transcontinental telephone line completed near Wendover?

**A.** 1914.

◆

**Q.** What town did a young widow, Isabell Birch Bryner, save from preemption by homesteaders in 1892 by traveling in a tent pitched on a boxcar to Salt Lake City to file a claim on the townsite?

**A.** Price.

◆

**Q.** In what year did Utah elect three representatives to the U.S. House of Representatives for the first time?

**A.** 1982.

**Q.** What women's college did Sister Madeleva, a Catholic poet, establish in Utah in the 1920s?

**A.** Saint Mary of the Wasatch.

---

**Q.** What group founded an agricultural colony in Keetley, between Park City and Heber City, during World War II?

**A.** Japanese Americans relocated from the West Coast.

---

**Q.** Who was the leading Jewish businesswoman in Utah in the 1860s and 1870s?

**A.** Isabella "Fanny" Brooks.

---

**Q.** What Salt Lake City native and leader of the radical Industrial Workers of the World is buried in the Kremlin Wall?

**A.** William D. "Big Bill" Haywood.

---

**Q.** What Indian language spoken in Utah is related to Apache?

**A.** Navajo.

---

**Q.** After arriving in Utah Territory on August 14, 1873, who spent the next forty years directing the growth of the Catholic community in Utah?

**A.** Father (later Bishop) Lawrence Scanlan.

---

**Q.** To what high office was Charles S. Zane elected in 1895 despite years of sending Mormon polygamists to prison?

**A.** Utah State Supreme Court justice.

**Q.** Residents of what town moved 15,000 feet of lumber from a snowbound sawmill, made 250,000 bricks, quarried stone, and completed a large building in nine months to keep its claim to a state college?

**A.** Cedar City.

---

**Q.** How long was the average handcart journey from Florence, Iowa, to Salt Lake City?

**A.** Sixty-five days.

---

**Q.** Which former U.S. senator from Utah was shot and killed by his mistress in 1906?

**A.** Arthur Brown.

---

**Q.** How many times did Franklin D. Roosevelt win Utah's electoral votes for the presidency?

**A.** Four (1932, 1936, 1940, and 1944).

---

**Q.** What conservative Utah Republican senator played a key role in the censure of Senator Joseph McCarthy?

**A.** Arthur V. Watkins.

---

**Q.** In what year did Utah elect two representatives to the U.S. House of Representatives for the first time?

**A.** 1912.

---

**Q.** What labor agent helped bring hundreds of Greek workers to Utah at the beginning of the twentieth century?

**A.** Leonidas Skliris.

**Q.** Against what groups were Ku Klux Klan activities directed in Utah during the 1920s?

**A.** Catholics and foreign-born immigrants.

———◆———

**Q.** What 1849 California-bound gold rusher persuaded several companions to attempt an unsuccessful trip down the Green River to reach California?

**A.** William Manly.

———◆———

**Q.** Who is known as "the Buckskin Apostle" for his missionary work among Indians in southern Utah?

**A.** Jacob Hamblin.

———◆———

**Q.** Between 1856 and 1860 how many handcarts were pulled from Iowa to the Salt Lake Valley?

**A.** 650 (accompanying approximately 3,000 people).

———◆———

**Q.** What is the oldest non-Mormon church building in Salt Lake City?

**A.** Saint Mark's Episcopal Cathedral (built in 1870).

———◆———

**Q.** In 1825 who were the first two white men known to have seen the Great Salt Lake?

**A.** Jim Bridger and Etienne Provost.

———◆———

**Q.** When did John Wesley Powell make his first voyage down the Green and Colorado Rivers?

**A.** 1869.

**Q.** What ethnic group predominated in the early years of Scofield?

**A.** Finns.

———◆———

**Q.** Where was the first fur trade rendezvous held in Utah?

**A.** Cache Valley (during the summer of 1826).

———◆———

**Q.** In 1996 the State Board of Regents named Grace Sawyer Jones, an African American, to head what college?

**A.** College of Eastern Utah.

———◆———

**Q.** What two women ran against each other for Congress in 1950?

**A.** Reva Beck Bosone, the winner, and Ivy Baker Priest.

———◆———

**Q.** Who reportedly promised Brigham Young a hundred dollars if the Mormons could raise a bushel of corn in the Salt Lake Valley?

**A.** Jim Bridger.

———◆———

**Q.** When was Brigham Young University established?

**A.** 1875.

———◆———

**Q.** Which five camps or forts were established by the U.S. Army in nineteenth-century Utah?

**A.** Camp Floyd (1858); Fort Douglas (1862); Fort Cameron (1872); Fort Thornburgh (1881); and Fort Duchesne (1886).

**Q.** What plant was built during World War II near Salt Lake City's Redwood Road to manufacture small arms and ammunition?

**A.** Remington Arms Plant.

---

**Q.** What former Utah governor served as secretary of war in Franklin D. Roosevelt's first cabinet?

**A.** George Dern.

---

**Q.** What Democrat defeated long-time U.S. senator Reed Smoot in 1932?

**A.** Elbert Thomas.

---

**Q.** As of 1997 who had been Utah's longest-serving member of the U.S. House of Representatives?

**A.** James V. Hansen (1980–).

---

**Q.** How many Democrats were elected to the Utah legislature in 1908?

**A.** Two, in the house of representatives (the senate was entirely Republican).

---

**Q.** In the 1912 presidential election, what candidate received the electoral votes of only two states, Utah and Vermont?

**A.** William Howard Taft.

---

**Q.** Who was the first female lieutenant governor elected in Utah?

**A.** Olene Walker (1992).

**Q.** Where were the fur trade rendezvous held in 1827 and in 1828?

**A.** South end of Bear Lake.

———◆———

**Q.** What was the largest nonmilitary, federally funded project in Utah during World War II?

**A.** Geneva Steel Plant.

———◆———

**Q.** What was the name given Mormon dissenters in the late 1860s and 1870s who, among other things, founded the *Salt Lake Tribune*?

**A.** The Godbeites.

———◆———

**Q.** The Hastings Cutoff through Utah saved how many miles for California-bound pioneers?

**A.** About two hundred.

———◆———

**Q.** What U.S. senator composes religious hymns and was once a member of the AFL-CIO?

**A.** Orrin Hatch.

———◆———

**Q.** What prominent Salt Lake City building was twice dynamited during its construction in 1910 by disgruntled union workers?

**A.** Hotel Utah (now the Joseph Smith Building).

———◆———

**Q.** Which Jewish congregation was organized in Utah in 1873?

**A.** Congregation B'nai Israel.

**Q.** What U.S. cavalry officer led the Utah Expedition against the Mormons in 1857?

**A.** Col. Albert Sidney Johnston (later a Confederate general who died at Shiloh).

**Q.** For whom is Judge Memorial High School, originally a hospital, named?

**A.** Park City mine owner John Judge.

**Q.** In 1992 who was elected governor, sixteen years after his father was defeated for the same office?

**A.** Michael Leavitt (his father, Dixie Leavitt, lost the 1976 election to Scott Matheson).

**Q.** Who served six terms as mayor of Price, three terms as mayor of Salt Lake City, and two terms as governor of Utah?

**A.** J. Bracken Lee.

**Q.** Who was the only person tried and executed for the infamous Mountain Meadows Massacre?

**A.** John D. Lee.

**Q.** What U.S. Supreme Court decision in 1897 upheld a Utah law prohibiting women and children from working in mines?

**A.** Holden v. Hardy.

**Q.** In what year did LDS Church president Wilford Woodruff publish the Manifesto, which ended the practice of polygamy?

**A.** 1890.

**Q.** To what Utah post were two companies of the Ninth Cavalry, an African-American unit, sent in 1886?

**A.** Fort Duchesne.

———◆———

**Q.** Who was the first woman elected a judge in Utah?

**A.** Reva Beck Bosone (1936).

———◆———

**Q.** When was the "This Is the Place" Monument erected near the mouth of Emigration Canyon?

**A.** 1947.

———◆———

**Q.** Who was the first representative to hold Utah's Third Congressional District seat?

**A.** Howard C. Nielson (elected to five terms beginning in 1982).

———◆———

**Q.** What mining town was almost completely destroyed by fire in 1898?

**A.** Park City.

———◆———

**Q.** What did the Morrill Act passed by Congress in 1862 prohibit?

**A.** Polygamy.

———◆———

**Q.** How long did the pony express operate?

**A.** Eighteen months (from April 1860 until October 1861).

**Q.** Robert Leroy Parker and Harry Longabaugh were better known by what nicknames?

**A.** Butch Cassidy and the Sundance Kid.

———◆———

**Q.** In what year did Utah establish statewide prohibition?

**A.** 1917.

———◆———

**Q.** The railroad came to Salt Lake City in what year?

**A.** 1870.

———◆———

**Q.** When was the first streetcar line established in Utah?

**A.** 1872 (in Salt Lake City).

———◆———

**Q.** Who was the first Utahn to serve a full six-year term as U.S. senator?

**A.** Joseph L. Rawlins.

———◆———

**Q.** What Ogden native served as secretary of education under Ronald Reagan?

**A.** Terrel H. Bell.

———◆———

**Q.** In 1898 the U.S. Congress refused to seat what Utah congressman because of his practice of polygamy?

**A.** Brigham H. Roberts.

**Q.** In what community were nine German prisoners of war killed and nineteen wounded by an army guard shortly after the end of World War II?

**A.** Salina.

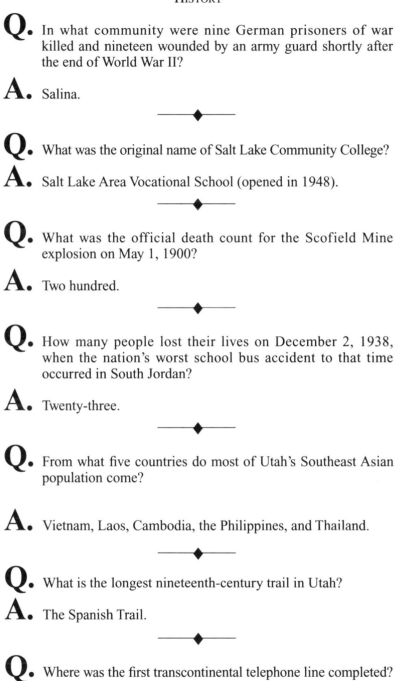

**Q.** What was the original name of Salt Lake Community College?

**A.** Salt Lake Area Vocational School (opened in 1948).

**Q.** What was the official death count for the Scofield Mine explosion on May 1, 1900?

**A.** Two hundred.

**Q.** How many people lost their lives on December 2, 1938, when the nation's worst school bus accident to that time occurred in South Jordan?

**A.** Twenty-three.

**Q.** From what five countries do most of Utah's Southeast Asian population come?

**A.** Vietnam, Laos, Cambodia, the Philippines, and Thailand.

**Q.** What is the longest nineteenth-century trail in Utah?

**A.** The Spanish Trail.

**Q.** Where was the first transcontinental telephone line completed?

**A.** Wendover, on the Utah-Nevada border (June 17, 1914).

**Q.** When was the Salt Lake Temple completed?

**A.** 1893.

---

**Q.** What prominent Utahn did George Wallace hope to have as his running mate on the American Party presidential ticket in 1968?

**A.** Ezra Taft Benson.

---

**Q.** What U.S. senator, fluent in Japanese, broadcast a monthly message to Japan in an effort to help end World War II?

**A.** Elbert D. Thomas.

---

**Q.** What was the fate of the battleship USS *Utah*?

**A.** It was sunk at Pearl Harbor on December 7, 1941.

---

**Q.** What is the state motto?

**A.** Industry.

---

**Q.** When did Utah Valley Community College move to its southwest Orem campus?

**A.** 1977.

---

**Q.** What disaster claimed twenty-seven lives on December 19, 1984?

**A.** Wilberg Mine disaster.

**Q.** What Brigham Young University president was an unsuccessful candidate for the U.S. senate?

**A.** Ernest L. Wilkinson.

**Q.** What name has been given to the movement by Utah and other western states to gain greater control over huge tracts of federal land within their borders?

**A.** Sagebrush Rebellion.

**Q.** What was the local name—initially of pioneer leather goods—for all home-manufactured items, including whiskey?

**A.** Valley Tan.

**Q.** How many tons of material are removed daily from Kennecott's Bingham Canyon Mine?

**A.** 320,000.

# ARTS & LITERATURE

C  H  A  P  T  E  R      F  O  U  R

---

**Q.** What Salt Lake City-born cartoonist produced classic portrayals of the era of the flapper, bootlegging, and jazz?

**A.** John Held Jr.

◆

**Q.** In what performing arts establishment did genre painter Dan Weggeland, who came to Utah in 1862, find work for over a decade?

**A.** Salt Lake Theatre.

◆

**Q.** Broadway actress Ada Dwyer of Utah influenced the career of what famous American poet?

**A.** Amy Lowell.

◆

**Q.** What Utah-born writer and lecturer is the author of, among other books, *The Seven Habits of Highly Effective People*?

**A.** Steven R. Covey.

◆

**Q.** What Utah composer's works include the music for *Saturday's Warrior*?

**A.** Lex de Azevedo.

**Q.** Harold Schindler's *Man of God, Son of Thunder* depicts the life of what Utah frontiersman?

**A.** Orrin Porter Rockwell.

---

**Q.** What popular cartoonist has published such books as *Faith Promoting Rumors* and *Freeway to Perfection*?

**A.** Calvin Grondahl.

---

**Q.** What high school building is one of the state's significant art deco structures?

**A.** Ogden High School.

---

**Q.** What prominent early Utah photographer founded Old Folks Day?

**A.** Charles R. Savage.

---

**Q.** Novelist Orson Scott Card, who has won both Hugo and Nebula Awards, is associated with what literary genre?

**A.** Science fiction.

---

**Q.** Which southeastern Utah canyon is one of the world's greatest prehistoric rock art sites?

**A.** Barrier or Horseshoe Canyon.

---

**Q.** What did Alma Compton of Brigham City produce forty thousand of during his career?

**A.** Photographs.

**Q.** What University of Utah professor won the Pulitzer Prize for poetry in 1986 for *The Flying Change*?

**A.** Henry Taylor.

———◆———

**Q.** In which town did Scottish stonemason Thomas Frazer build numerous homes now listed in the National Register of Historic Places?

**A.** Beaver.

———◆———

**Q.** What American writer described his first glimpse of Salt Lake City in 1861 as "a child's toy village reposing under the majestic protection of the Chinese wall"?

**A.** Mark Twain (in *Roughing It*).

———◆———

**Q.** Who carved the lion for Brigham Young's Lion House?

**A.** William Ward.

———◆———

**Q.** What long-time president of the Daughters of Utah Pioneers supervised the compilation of numerous volumes of Utah history?

**A.** Kate B. Carter.

———◆———

**Q.** Norman Mailer's Pulitzer Prize-winning novel, *The Executioner's Song,* was based on the life of what Utah murderer?

**A.** Gary Gilmore.

———◆———

**Q.** Taylor Woolley studied under what famous architect, helping to prepare the influential Wasmuth Portfolio for publication?

**A.** Frank Lloyd Wright.

**Q.** Where was Handel's *Messiah* first performed in the area between Chicago and the West Coast?

**A.** Salt Lake Theatre, June 3, 1875.

---

**Q.** Where did the Military Dramatic Association begin to produce plays in the fall of 1858?

**A.** Camp Floyd.

---

**Q.** Who built the first organ in Utah, for the Salt Lake Tabernacle?

**A.** Joseph H. Ridges.

---

**Q.** What former Logan resident and presidential candidate wrote *From Housewife to Heretic*?

**A.** Sonia Johnson.

---

**Q.** What major musical organization in Utah is second only to the Mormon Tabernacle Choir in number of years of continuous performances?

**A.** Oratorio Society of Utah.

---

**Q.** What is depicted by a dramatic bronze sculpture outside the Prehistoric Museum at the College of Eastern Utah?

**A.** Two dinosaurs fighting.

---

**Q.** Whose autobiography is titled *A Mormon Mother*?

**A.** Annie Clark Tanner.

**Q.** What author, who wrote *Desert Solitaire* and *The Monkey Wrench Gang,* worked for the National Park Service at Arches?

**A.** Edward Abbey.

———◆———

**Q.** Who is considered the most prolific and influential twentieth-century historian of Mormonism?

**A.** Leonard J. Arrington.

———◆———

**Q.** In what resort town can one find the Kimball Art Center?

**A.** Park City.

———◆———

**Q.** Who conducted the first Utah performance of Handel's *Messiah*?

**A.** George Careless.

———◆———

**Q.** As of 1996 what native of Wales was poet-in-residence at Brigham Young University?

**A.** Leslie Norris.

———◆———

**Q.** What Salt Lake City opera house, built by a famous merchant family, was destroyed by fire on July 3, 1890?

**A.** Walker Opera House.

———◆———

**Q.** Which niece of the Mormon prophet Joseph Smith became California's first poet laureate?

**A.** Ina Coolbrith (Josephine Donna Smith).

**Q.** Who, in addition to editing the *Young Woman's Journal* and the *Relief Society Magazine,* was one of Utah's most prolific writers?

**A.** Susa Young Gates.

———◆———

**Q.** What artist, known for his portrait of Chief Walker, accompanied Frémont's fifth expedition?

**A.** Solomon N. Carvalho.

———◆———

**Q.** What Provo native wrote *A Daughter of Zion* and *A House of Many Rooms*?

**A.** Rodello Hunter.

———◆———

**Q.** Which southern Utah town, settled in 1851, is considered by folklorists to have the most impressive gravestone art?

**A.** Parowan.

———◆———

**Q.** Through many remodelings, what Salt Lake City building has preserved its historic 1875–76 cast-iron facade, designed by architect William H. Folsom?

**A.** ZCMI.

———◆———

**Q.** How many pipes are in the present organ in the Mormon Tabernacle in Salt Lake City?

**A.** 11,623.

———◆———

**Q.** What poetic government geologist wrote, "The Aquarius [Plateau] should be described in blank verse and illustrated upon a canvas"?

**A.** Clarence E. Dutton.

**Q.** What is Utah's premier international musical event?

**A.** Gina Bachauer International Piano Competition.

---

**Q.** What theatrical superstar commanded a weekly salary of three hundred dollars when she thrilled Utah audiences during an extended engagement from August 1865 to June 1866?

**A.** Julia Dean Hayne.

---

**Q.** Sculptor Cyrus E. Dallin's work *Pioneer Mother Monument* is in which Utah city?

**A.** Springville (Civic Center Park).

---

**Q.** Commuting from Hollywood in 1946, who conducted the modern Utah Symphony in its first season?

**A.** Werner Janssen.

---

**Q.** Who wrote *Children of Covenant,* a novel set in Ogden?

**A.** Richard Scowcroft.

---

**Q.** What Shakespearean play, first produced in Utah on January 4, 1865, featured one hundred voices from the Mormon Tabernacle Choir?

**A.** *Macbeth* (the choir sang the witches' part).

---

**Q.** Who painted the mural in the Union Pacific Depot in Salt Lake City, depicting the arrival of the pioneers in July 1847?

**A.** John McQuarrie.

**Q.** What did Joseph J. Daynes, Frank W. Asper, and Alexander Schreiner have in common?

**A.** All were Mormon Tabernacle organists.

◆

**Q.** What nineteenth-century American author wrote of the adventures of Captain B. L. E. Bonneville, for whom Lake Bonneville was named?

**A.** Washington Irving.

◆

**Q.** Who founded the Oratorio Society of Utah in 1914?

**A.** Squire Coop.

◆

**Q.** Actress Annie Kiskadden was the mother of what more famous actress of the Utah and Broadway stage?

**A.** Maude Adams.

◆

**Q.** What Salt Lake City native published *Yank* magazine for the army during World War II, put *Mademoiselle* on a sound financial footing, and also published *Liberty* and *Charm* magazines?

**A.** Franklin S. Forsberg.

◆

**Q.** Who was the first director of the Salt Lake Theatre Orchestra?

**A.** Charles J. Thomas.

◆

**Q.** Who created the nationally acclaimed Children's Dance Theatre?

**A.** Virginia Tanner.

**Q.** What Utah historian published *The Mountain Meadows Massacre* in 1950, a book about a controversial Utah tragedy?

**A.** Juanita Brooks.

---

**Q.** What Utah sculptor, also a published poet, is widely known for works that include children at play?

**A.** Dennis Smith.

---

**Q.** Who wrote *Wife No. 19,* the story of her marriage to Brigham Young?

**A.** Ann Eliza Webb Young.

---

**Q.** What newspaper did Kuniko M. Terasawa continue to publish for fifty-two years following the death of her husband in 1939?

**A.** The *Utah Nippo.*

---

**Q.** What two professional modern dance companies are in Salt Lake City?

**A.** Repertory Dance Theatre and Ririe-Woodbury Dance Company.

---

**Q.** Most of Lorenzo Dow Young's journal of the 1847 pioneer trek to Utah was actually written by whom?

**A.** Harriet Decker Young, his wife.

---

**Q.** What Utah painter and teacher is especially known for his large murals in the Salt Lake City Public Library and other buildings?

**A.** V. Douglas Snow.

**Q.** Which Utah governor was a published poet?

**A.** Charles R. Mabey.

---

**Q.** Who founded Pioneer Craft House in the 1950s in Salt Lake City?

**A.** Glenn Beeley.

---

**Q.** What subject matter is especially associated with Clark Bronson's watercolors and sculptures?

**A.** Wildlife.

---

**Q.** The sculptor of Mount Rushmore, Gutzon Borglum, lived in which Utah city after his family moved from Saint Charles, Idaho?

**A.** Ogden.

---

**Q.** The University of Utah was the first college in the United States to establish a major in what performing art?

**A.** Ballet.

---

**Q.** Harold Ross, founder of *New Yorker* magazine, attended which Salt Lake City high school?

**A.** West High School.

---

**Q.** What musical organization performs at Deer Valley and Snowbird in the summer?

**A.** Utah Symphony.

**Q.** What annual summer workshop brings publishers and authors to Park City?

**A.** Writers at Work.

---

**Q.** Annual exhibits of local artists began to be sponsored in 1856 by the Deseret Agriculture and Manufacturing Society, a forerunner of what present organization?

**A.** Utah State Fair.

---

**Q.** Who is the central historical figure in the 1950 novel *The Preacher and the Slave* by University of Utah graduate Wallace Stegner?

**A.** Joe Hill.

---

**Q.** In what city is the Ellen Eccles Theatre?

**A.** Logan.

---

**Q.** What native of Fountain Green, who made his first violin from a cigar box, composed *Passacaglia for Orchestra,* the prize-winning *Trilogy,* and *Oratorio from the Book of Mormon*?

**A.** Leroy Robertson.

---

**Q.** Navajo artisans are especially associated with what two crafts?

**A.** Silversmithing and weaving.

---

**Q.** The history of which major immigrant group in Utah is depicted in the 1970 landmark study *Toil and Rage in a New Land*?

**A.** Greeks.

**Q.** What tenor was the founding director of the Utah Opera Company?

**A.** Glade Peterson.

◆

**Q.** Whose 1776 diary is one of the first documents in Utah history?

**A.** Father Silvestre Velez de Escalante.

◆

**Q.** What sculpture did Ralph Ramsay carve and assemble from five separate pieces of wood in 1859?

**A.** *Eagle for Eagle Gate.*

◆

**Q.** Landscape painter John Hafen was a native of what country?

**A.** Switzerland.

◆

**Q.** For what traditional Japanese artistic skill did Mrs. Izyo Kiyoshi Sauki (Madame Ogyoku) gain recognition as both a practitioner and a teacher?

**A.** Flower arranging.

◆

**Q.** What popular writer of westerns, including *Riders of the Purple Sage,* gave Mormonism a sensational twist in some novels?

**A.** Zane Grey.

◆

**Q.** What youthful letter writer, watercolorist, and adventurer mysteriously disappeared into the Utah wilderness in November 1934?

**A.** Everett Reuss.

**Q.** In 1984 who wrote *In My Father's House,* a frank look at contemporary polygamy?

**A.** Dorothy Allred Solomon.

———◆———

**Q.** What native of Staffordshire, England, was called "the poet laureate of Dixie" by settlers in southwestern Utah?

**A.** Charles Lowell Walker.

———◆———

**Q.** What newspaper was first issued on June 15, 1850?

**A.** *Deseret News.*

———◆———

**Q.** What mystery writer sets many of his novels on the Navajo Reservation?

**A.** Tony Hillerman.

———◆———

**Q.** What artist began in 1878 to paint large murals that could be rolled up to use in relating the history of the Mormons?

**A.** C. C. A. Christensen.

———◆———

**Q.** In *Our Inland Sea,* what early artist-writer described his fourteen-month stay on Gunnison Island?

**A.** Alfred Lambourne.

———◆———

**Q.** What two points of view were represented in what J. Cecil Alter called "a half-century of forensic warfare, waged by the West's most militant Press"?

**A.** Mormon and anti-Mormon.

**Q.** In the early 1900s the Silver Queen built a large structure for social events and to house art works next to what home originally owned by Brigham Young?

**A.** Gardo House, or Amelia's Palace.

---

**Q.** What Utah artist created murals in the Price Municipal Building and in the visitors center at the "This Is the Place" Monument?

**A.** Lynn Fausett.

---

**Q.** Topaz in Millard County is the setting of *Desert Exile: The Uprooting of a Japanese American Family,* written in 1982 by what author?

**A.** Yoshiko Uchida.

---

**Q.** What former Utah schoolteacher founded Reading Dynamics, an internationally used technique for speed-reading?

**A.** Evelyn Wood.

---

**Q.** In 1882 Marie Gorlinski became the first Utah artist to travel to what city to study?

**A.** Paris.

---

**Q.** Which novel by Sir Arthur Conan Doyle features a sensational Mormon polygamy plot?

**A.** *A Study in Scarlet.*

---

**Q.** Composer, musician, and linguist Gerrit de Jong Jr., who established Brigham Young University's College of Fine Arts, was a native of what country?

**A.** The Netherlands.

**Q.** The naturalist-in-residence at the Utah Museum of Natural History, University of Utah, is what writer of such nonfiction works as *Coyote's Canyon* and *Refuge*?

**A.** Terry Tempest Williams.

---

**Q.** During 1890–92 what organization sent several Utah artists, including John Hafen and Edwin Evans, to Paris to study painting?

**A.** LDS Church.

---

**Q.** Sheepherder Sam, a popular cartoon character in the *Salt Lake Tribune,* was created in 1952 by Chris Jensen, a Danish-born resident of which Sanpete County town?

**A.** Ephraim.

---

**Q.** Wallace Thurman, an African-American writer of the 1920s and 1930s and author of *The Blacker the Berry,* was born in which Utah city?

**A.** Salt Lake City.

---

**Q.** Who was the first Utah artist to have a painting exhibited at the Paris Salon?

**A.** James T. Harwood (1892).

---

**Q.** Newspapers were published in Utah in what six foreign languages in the early decades of the twentieth century?

**A.** Danish, German, Japanese, Greek, Swedish, and Norwegian.

---

**Q.** Which sculptor won recognition for his small figures of boxers and laborers as well as for the *Seagull* and "This Is the Place" monuments?

**A.** Mahonri M. Young.

**Q.** Which Ute dance is traditionally held in the spring?

**A.** Bear Dance.

———◆———

**Q.** Artist Lee Greene Richards was in charge of the painting of murals in which public building in Salt Lake City?

**A.** Utah State Capitol.

———◆———

**Q.** Which Brigham City native has been called "the father of Utah ballet"?

**A.** Willam F. "Bill" Christensen.

———◆———

**Q.** Who wrote a fictional account of the Mormons, *Children of God,* that won the 1939 Harper Prize?

**A.** Vardis Fisher.

———◆———

**Q.** What small arts facility on Finch Lane near the University of Utah was dedicated on June 11, 1933?

**A.** Art Barn.

———◆———

**Q.** What sculptor of works depicting LDS history and the first dean of the College of Fine Arts at the University of Utah helped to make nude figures acceptable to local museum-goers?

**A.** Avard Fairbanks.

———◆———

**Q.** Children's books author Olive Woolley Burt published a collection of what unusual kind of storytelling songs?

**A.** Murder ballads.

**Q.** What was the new name given the Utah Civic Ballet in 1968 to reflect its regional scope?

**A.** Ballet West.

◆

**Q.** Who wrote *Utah, the Right Place,* the official Utah statehood centennial history?

**A.** Thomas G. Alexander.

◆

**Q.** Where in Utah County did George Edward Anderson, a photographer who documented many aspects of life in Utah, have his studio?

**A.** Springville.

◆

**Q.** What state-of-the-art facility opened in 1993 with a major exhibit of Etruscan art and artifacts from the Vatican?

**A.** Museum of Art at Brigham Young University.

◆

**Q.** Which German-born architect designed the Utah State Capitol?

**A.** Richard K. A. Kletting.

◆

**Q.** Who grew up in Manti, wrote novels such as *Where Nothing Is Long Ago,* received two Guggenheim Fellowships, and married English writer Alec Waugh?

**A.** Virginia Sorensen.

◆

**Q.** What artist and teacher, known especially for his rural landscapes, remained an active painter well into his nineties, dying in Kaysville in 1990?

**A.** LeConte Stewart.

**Q.** Who painted two large murals in Kingsbury Hall at the University of Utah in 1937 depicting "the whole history of the arts in the western world"?

**A.** Florence Ware.

◆

**Q.** Which German-born architect designed the Governor's (Kearns) Mansion?

**A.** Carl M. Neuhausen.

◆

**Q.** In 1915 soprano Emma Lucy Gates, granddaughter of Brigham Young, founded and directed what touring arts group?

**A.** Lucy Gates Grand Opera Company.

◆

**Q.** What Utah-based periodical for women was founded in 1872?

**A.** *Woman's Exponent.*

◆

**Q.** J. Cecil Alter, founding editor in 1928 of the *Utah Historical Quarterly,* held what federal position in Salt Lake City for many years?

**A.** Chief of the National Weather Service regional office.

◆

**Q.** In which east-central Utah town was John Dennis Fitzgerald, creator of the popular Great Brain Series for juvenile readers, born and raised?

**A.** Price.

◆

**Q.** Phyllis McGinley, who won a Pulitzer Prize in 1961 for her book of light verse, *Times Three,* graduated from which Utah high school?

**A.** Ogden High School.

**Q.** What American Fork native and BYU professor has been credited with ushering Mormon poetry into the modern era?

**A.** Clinton F. Larson.

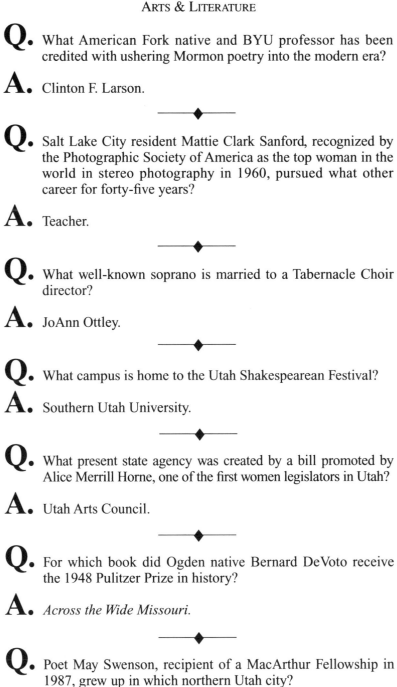

**Q.** Salt Lake City resident Mattie Clark Sanford, recognized by the Photographic Society of America as the top woman in the world in stereo photography in 1960, pursued what other career for forty-five years?

**A.** Teacher.

**Q.** What well-known soprano is married to a Tabernacle Choir director?

**A.** JoAnn Ottley.

**Q.** What campus is home to the Utah Shakespearean Festival?

**A.** Southern Utah University.

**Q.** What present state agency was created by a bill promoted by Alice Merrill Horne, one of the first women legislators in Utah?

**A.** Utah Arts Council.

**Q.** For which book did Ogden native Bernard DeVoto receive the 1948 Pulitzer Prize in history?

**A.** *Across the Wide Missouri.*

**Q.** Poet May Swenson, recipient of a MacArthur Fellowship in 1987, grew up in which northern Utah city?

**A.** Logan.

**Q.** Who wrote *The Giant Joshua,* published in 1941 and called by some critics "the finest Mormon novel to date"?

**A.** Maurine Whipple.

---

**Q.** Mark Strand, poet laureate of the United States during 1990–91, taught at which Utah university?

**A.** University of Utah.

---

**Q.** For what kind of fiction is Utahn Barbara Williams known?

**A.** Juvenile.

---

**Q.** On what sacred Indian ceremony did Will Hanson, a Uintah High School music teacher, and Gertrude Bonnin, a musician and Sioux Indian, base a successful opera in 1913?

**A.** Sun Dance.

---

**Q.** Deaf from age four, Elfie Huntington of Springville produced a large body of highly regarded creative work in what artistic medium?

**A.** Photography.

---

**Q.** As a result of their interest in orthographic reform, what did the Mormons create?

**A.** Deseret alphabet.

---

**Q.** The *Broad Ax* and the *Plain Dealer,* two turn-of-the-century Salt Lake City newspapers, served which ethnic community?

**A.** African-American.

**Q.** What Broadway star of light opera and musical comedy, who often played opposite Al Jolson, retired to her native Utah in 1937?

**A.** Viola Gillette.

---

**Q.** What three figures are depicted on top of the "This Is the Place" Monument?

**A.** Brigham Young, Heber C. Kimball, and Wilford Woodruff.

---

**Q.** What Utah town is nicknamed Art City?

**A.** Springville.

---

**Q.** Who wrote the words to "Come, Come, Ye Saints," perhaps the most famous Mormon hymn?

**A.** William Clayton.

---

**Q.** An important setting in Tony Hillerman's novel *A Thief of Time* is what southeastern Utah lodge?

**A.** Recapture Lodge in Bluff.

---

**Q.** Who is the founder of the Utah Shakespearean Festival?

**A.** Fred Adams.

---

**Q.** What Utah community was named for the subject of a famous poem by Henry Wadsworth Longfellow?

**A.** Hiawatha, Carbon County.

**Q.** Who was conductor of the Utah Symphony from 1947 to 1979?

**A.** Maurice Abravanel.

———◆———

**Q.** Who designed the Salt Lake Temple?

**A.** Truman Angell.

———◆———

**Q.** What architect was named the first fellow of the Utah Chapter of the American Institute of Architects?

**A.** Walter E. Ware.

———◆———

**Q.** What Utah-founded group was the only successful repertory theater company in the western United States in the 1920s?

**A.** Moroni Olsen Players.

———◆———

**Q.** Who is considered Utah's first lady of the theater?

**A.** Maud May Babcock.

———◆———

**Q.** What Utahn wrote controversial biographies of Joseph Smith, Thomas Jefferson, and Richard Nixon using psychological techniques to probe character?

**A.** Fawn McKay Brodie.

———◆———

**Q.** What community was the location of a bitter battle in the early 1970s to save its most prominent historic landmark?

**A.** Coalville (LDS Tabernacle).

**Q.** What Springfield native sculpted Angel Moroni atop the Salt Lake Temple, the Brigham Young Monument, and Chief Massossoit in front of the Utah State Capitol?

**A.** Cyrus E. Dallin.

———◆———

**Q.** What husband and wife team helped pioneer the study of folklore in Utah with such works as *Saints of Sage and Saddle: Folklore among the Mormons*?

**A.** Austin and Alta Fife.

———◆———

**Q.** Who became the best-known Salt Lake Tabernacle organist after he immigrated to Utah from Nuremberg, Germany, in 1912?

**A.** Alexander Schreiner.

———◆———

**Q.** When was the *Salt Lake Tribune* founded?

**A.** 1870.

———◆———

**Q.** Whose diary is considered to be one of the best personal accounts of the 1850–56 period in Utah?

**A.** Martha Spence Heywood.

———◆———

**Q.** What former "Danite" (member of a secretive vigilante group) published his autobiography, *Brigham's Destroying Angel,* in 1872?

**A.** William A. Hickman.

———◆———

**Q.** What songwriter and organizer for the radical labor movement the Industrial Workers of the World was executed in Utah?

**A.** Joe Hill.

**Q.** What Danish-born historian authored and edited more than thirty books, including the four-volume *L.D.S. Biographical Encyclopedia*?

**A.** Andrew Jenson.

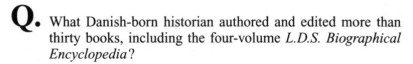

**Q.** What Mormon scholar, known for his humorous stories and colorful language, has been studied by folklorists and is the subject of a one-man theater production?

**A.** J. Golden Kimball.

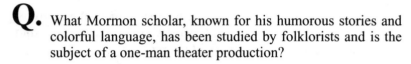

**Q.** What Utah community is the subject of Edward Geary's *Goodbye to Poplarhaven*?

**A.** Huntington, Emery County.

**Q.** Which two Wallace Stegner novels are set in Utah?

**A.** *The Big Rock Candy Mountain* and *Recapitulation.*

**Q.** Who wrote *Small Bird Tell Me* and *The Apple Falls from the Apple Tree,* collections of short stories about Greek immigrants and their children in Utah?

**A.** Helen Zeese Papanikolas.

**Q.** What three kinds of local stone did Utah pioneer builders use?

**A.** Granite, limestone, and sandstone.

**Q.** What Utah-born historian wrote *The Great Salt Lake* and *Jedediah Smith and the Opening of the West*?

**A.** Dale L. Morgan.

**Q.** What two monuments on the State Capitol grounds commemorate military events that did not take place in Utah?

**A.** Mormon Battalion Monument and Vietnam Memorial.

◆

**Q.** In 1937 what art museum was constructed under a New Deal program?

**A.** Springville Museum of Art.

◆

**Q.** The title of what novel by Zane Grey is a Utah landmark?

**A.** *Rainbow Bridge.*

◆

**Q.** What poet and acknowledged leader of Mormon pioneer women wrote nine books?

**A.** Eliza Roxcy Snow.

◆

**Q.** The Mormon Tabernacle Choir began its ongoing weekly radio broadcasts on what date?

**A.** July 15, 1929.

◆

**Q.** What event do the figures on the south side of the "This Is the Place" Monument depict?

**A.** The 1776 Dominguez-Escalante expedition.

◆

**Q.** Wilburn C. West was the first full-time director of what state arts organization?

**A.** The Utah Arts Council.

**Q.** What private not-for-profit historic preservation organization was established in 1966?

**A.** Utah Heritage Foundation.

—◆—

**Q.** What historian and former university professor was the author of *Utah, A Bicentennial History*?

**A.** Charles S. Peterson.

—◆—

**Q.** What is the overall title of Gerald N. Lund's popular ongoing series of novels detailing the Mormon experience?

**A.** *The Work and the Glory.*

—◆—

**Q.** Who is the first director of the Utah Humanities Council?

**A.** Delmont R. Oswald.

—◆—

**Q.** What immense sculpture, representative of the earth art movement, was built at the north end of the Great Salt Lake in 1970 by Robert Smithson?

**A.** *The Spiral Jetty.*

—◆—

**Q.** What Utahn composed the Christmas song "Far, Far Away on Judea's Plain"?

**A.** William Baird.

—◆—

**Q.** What are the first two lines of Utah's state song?

**A.** "Land of the mountains high, Utah, we love thee!
Land of the sunny sky, Utah, we love thee!"

**Q.** The name of which small Cache County town brings William Shakespeare to mind?

**A.** Avon (named for the bard's birthplace).

———◆———

**Q.** What performing group has fostered the preservation and presentation of pioneer Utah music?

**A.** Deseret String Band.

———◆———

**Q.** Who wrote *Polygamy Was Better than Monotony*?

**A.** Paul D. Bailey.

———◆———

**Q.** What widely published University of Utah poet wrote *The Creative Process*?

**A.** Brewster Ghiselin.

———◆———

**Q.** The Madeleine Arts Festival is hosted by what organization?

**A.** Catholic Church (Cathedral of the Madeleine).

———◆———

**Q.** What native of Chile has exerted a powerful influence on Hispanic literature in Utah?

**A.** Hector Ahumada.

———◆———

**Q.** What Utah pianist began his professional concert career in 1944?

**A.** Grant Johannesen.

**Q.** What Utah painter, known for his widely reproduced illustrations of such subjects as Royal Canadian Mounted Police won an Oscar nomination for his design work for *The Ten Commandments*?

**A.** Arnold Friberg.

———◆———

**Q.** In 1990 what BYU faculty member and noted humorist wrote *Only When I Laugh*?

**A.** Eloise M. Bell.

———◆———

**Q.** What literary critic and theorist, who wrote *The Art of Modern Fiction* in 1949, was born in Logan?

**A.** Ray B. West Jr.

———◆———

**Q.** What publication has as its subtitle *A Journal of Mormon Thought*?

**A.** *Dialogue.*

———◆———

**Q.** What is the setting for *The Monkey Wrench Gang*?

**A.** Southeastern Utah.

———◆———

**Q.** Who designed the *Tree of Utah* on Interstate 80 about twenty-five miles east of Wendover?

**A.** Karl Momen.

———◆———

**Q.** Where is the Mormon Miracle Pageant performed each summer?

**A.** Manti.

# SPORTS & LEISURE

**Q.** Who is the only Utah college player to win college football's Heisman Trophy?

**A.** Ty Detmer (BYU quarterback, 1990).

———◆———

**Q.** Seven-foot, six-inch NBA basketball star Shawn Bradley attended what high school?

**A.** Emery County High School.

———◆———

**Q.** In what year did Brigham Young University win the NCAA football national championship?

**A.** 1984.

———◆———

**Q.** As of 1995, how many national championships had the University of Utah women's gymnastics team won?

**A.** Ten.

———◆———

**Q.** LaVell Edwards became head football coach at BYU in what year?

**A.** 1972.

**Q.** Who is considered to be the father of Utah skiing?

**A.** Alf Engen.

---

**Q.** In the 1950s, Salt Lake City's professional football team was known by what name?

**A.** Seagulls.

---

**Q.** The name of what state park might conjure up thoughts of Halloween?

**A.** Goblin Valley.

---

**Q.** What is the oldest and most popular mountain biking trail in Utah?

**A.** Slickrock Trail, near Moab.

---

**Q.** What difficult route taken by Mormon pioneers to reach the San Juan River in 1880 is now a popular recreation trail?

**A.** Hole-in-the-Rock Trail.

---

**Q.** Two of the most important attractions in what town are a former winery and a rock to which prisoners were chained because the community had no jail?

**A.** Toquerville.

---

**Q.** Arches National Park contains how many arches?

**A.** More than two thousand, with more discovered each year.

**Q.** What was the site of early ski-jumping demonstrations and competitions?

**A.** Ecker Hill.

———◆———

**Q.** What area of the Navajo Reservation has scenery rivaling that found in Utah's national parks?

**A.** Monument Valley.

———◆———

**Q.** When did the Lagoon Amusement Park open?

**A.** 1896.

———◆———

**Q.** Before it closed in 1987, what was Salt Lake City's most prestigious hotel?

**A.** Hotel Utah.

———◆———

**Q.** What was the first professional basketball team in Utah?

**A.** Utah Stars of the ABA (1971).

———◆———

**Q.** When did Utah's first chairlift go into operation?

**A.** January 15, 1939 (at Alta).

———◆———

**Q.** What is the term often applied to those who spend the fall and winter in southern Utah and return to their homes in the north in the spring?

**A.** Snowbirds.

**Q.** Who led the successful movement to have Columbus Day established as a state holiday in 1919?

**A.** Fortunato Anselmo (the Italian vice-consul in Utah).

---

**Q.** What is the length of the shoreline of Lake Powell, one of Utah's most popular recreation areas?

**A.** 1,960 miles.

---

**Q.** When did BYU win its first WAC football championship?

**A.** 1974.

---

**Q.** What 1959 University of Utah graduate was the first Utah college player inducted into the Pro Football Hall of Fame?

**A.** Larry Wilson.

---

**Q.** What Utahn is considered the inventor of the drive-in restaurant?

**A.** John Willard Marriott.

---

**Q.** When did the Delta Center open?

**A.** 1991.

---

**Q.** Where was Luke's Hot Pots Resort situated?

**A.** Midway in Heber Valley.

**Q.** In which canyon are the Alta and Snowbird ski resorts?

**A.** Little Cottonwood.

◆

**Q.** Utah's first museum, the Salt Lake City Museum and Menagerie, was established in what year?

**A.** 1869.

◆

**Q.** What city has held the Ute Stampede rodeo since 1936?

**A.** Nephi.

◆

**Q.** Highway 12 Scenic Byway runs between which two towns?

**A.** Panguitch and Torrey.

◆

**Q.** In what sport did BYU's Elwood Romney attain All-American status in the 1930s?

**A.** Basketball.

◆

**Q.** What Utahn owned the first Kentucky Fried Chicken franchise in the United States, still at its original location?

**A.** Leon "Pete" Harman.

◆

**Q.** The Park City Mining Adventure can be found in what historic mine?

**A.** Ontario Mine.

**Q.** In what year did Snow College win the Division II football national championship?

**A.** 1985.

---

**Q.** What was the first year that a BYU football team defeated the University of Utah?

**A.** 1942 (having tied the Utes in 1929).

---

**Q.** In what year did the Snowbird ski resort open?

**A.** 1972.

---

**Q.** When did the NBA's New Orleans Jazz move to Utah?

**A.** 1979.

---

**Q.** In what sport is Alvaro Palacios a champion?

**A.** Marathon running.

---

**Q.** In what event did Chad Bedell of Jensen win a world championship and $120,783 on December 15, 1996?

**A.** Steer wrestling (National Finals Rodeo in Las Vegas).

---

**Q.** What is the capacity of Snowbird's aerial tram?

**A.** 120 passengers.

**Q.** What Sanpete County town is listed in the National Register of Historic Places as one of the best preserved nineteenth-century Mormon villages?

**A.** Spring City.

---

**Q.** How tall is the wall around Temple Square?

**A.** Fifteen feet.

---

**Q.** When was Timpanogos Cave designated a national monument?

**A.** 1922.

---

**Q.** Who was the first Utah Jazz player to be named to the NBA All-Star team?

**A.** Adrian Dantley.

---

**Q.** In what sport was BYU sophomore Shauna Rohbock named to an All-America second team in December 1996, the first Cougar woman to win such an honor?

**A.** Soccer.

---

**Q.** Ogden's George Garcia created a giant version of what devotional object in 1996 by using bowling balls?

**A.** Rosary.

---

**Q.** In what year was the NBA All-Star game played in the Delta Center?

**A.** 1992.

**Q.** When was Utah's Fairpark, originally called Fair Grounds, established?

**A.** 1902.

---

**Q.** What Super Bowl-winning NFL coach played college football at the University of Utah and coached football at Westminster College?

**A.** George Siefert.

---

**Q.** Where can one find "Walter's Wiggles"?

**A.** Zion National Park.

---

**Q.** Near what city is the Elk Meadows ski resort?

**A.** Beaver.

---

**Q.** What are the three ski resorts in the Park City area?

**A.** Park City, Wolf Mountain, and Deer Valley.

---

**Q.** What BYU football player won the 1986 Outland Trophy as the nation's best defensive lineman?

**A.** Jason Buck.

---

**Q.** Where is the Great White Throne?

**A.** Zion National Park.

**Q.** For whom was Bryce Canyon named?

**A.** Ebenezer Bryce.

---

**Q.** The Bicentennial Highway connects which two Utah towns?

**A.** Hanksville and Blanding.

---

**Q.** The Burr Trail connects what two locations?

**A.** Boulder and the Bullfrog Marina at Lake Powell.

---

**Q.** What is the best-known arch in Arches National Park?

**A.** Delicate.

---

**Q.** Which two Utah state parks are named for prehistoric inhabitants of the area?

**A.** Fremont and Anasazi.

---

**Q.** What canyon in Capitol Reef National Park has ties to the nineteenth-century practice of polygamy?

**A.** Cohab.

---

**Q.** What Morgan County recreation area was named for the northern Italian birthplace of one of its residents?

**A.** Como Springs (Lake Como).

**Q.** BYU defeated what school in the first college football game broadcast live by ESPN in 1984?

**A.** University of Pittsburgh.

———◆———

**Q.** Created in 1996, what is Utah's newest national monument?

**A.** Grand Staircase-Escalante.

———◆———

**Q.** What basketball player was a member of both the Utah Stars and the Utah Jazz?

**A.** Ron Boone.

———◆———

**Q.** Who was the second BYU football player to win the Outland Trophy?

**A.** Moe Elewonibi.

———◆———

**Q.** Soldiers of the Tenth Mountain Division used what Utah ski resort for training during World War II?

**A.** Alta.

———◆———

**Q.** What former University of Utah basketball player was named the NBA All-Star Most Valuable Player in 1987?

**A.** Tom Chambers.

———◆———

**Q.** What is Karl Malone's jersey number?

**A.** 32.

**Q.** What Olympic gold-medal-winning skier is most closely associated with Deer Valley?

**A.** Stein Eriksen.

———◆———

**Q.** What Utah Jazz player is the all-time NBA leader in assists?

**A.** John Stockton.

———◆———

**Q.** When did Hot Rod Hundley begin his broadcasting career with the Utah Jazz?

**A.** 1974.

———◆———

**Q.** The University of Utah football team played in its first post-season bowl game in what year?

**A.** 1964 (Liberty Bowl, defeating West Virginia, 32-6).

———◆———

**Q.** Who is Utah's most famous cookie maker?

**A.** Debbi Fields.

———◆———

**Q.** The Utah Jazz appeared in their first postseason playoff in what year?

**A.** 1984.

———◆———

**Q.** What Utahn pitched for the Boston Red Sox in the 1986 World Series?

**A.** Bruce Hurst.

**Q.** What Utah resident was named Miss America in 1985 and later became an ESPN sports commentator?

**A.** Sharlene Wells (Hawkes).

---

**Q.** What Springville High School and University of Utah quarterback played for the Detroit Lions?

**A.** Scott Mitchell.

---

**Q.** What West Jordan boxer was world middleweight champion?

**A.** Gene Fullmer.

---

**Q.** Where are the Utah Summer Games held?

**A.** Cedar City.

---

**Q.** In what year was Salt Lake City chosen to host the 2002 Winter Olympics?

**A.** 1995.

---

**Q.** What Salt Lake City native managed the Chicago Cubs and the San Francisco Giants?

**A.** Herman Franks.

---

**Q.** In 1961 Enid Cosgriff became the first woman president and general manager of what kind of sports organization?

**A.** Professional baseball team (Salt Lake Bees).

**Q.** What museum in Logan portrays Utah farm life during the first decades of the twentieth century?

**A.** Ronald B. Jensen Living Historical Farm.

---

**Q.** When was the first baseball game played at Franklin Quest Field?

**A.** April 11, 1994.

---

**Q.** Whose coaching career includes Utah State University, Brigham Young University, and the Utah Jazz?

**A.** LaDell Anderson.

---

**Q.** What university is sometimes described as a quarterback factory for the NFL?

**A.** Brigham Young.

---

**Q.** Before it was changed to Rice Stadium, what was the name of the University of Utah's football stadium?

**A.** Ute Stadium.

---

**Q.** What town hosts Scandinavian Days in May?

**A.** Ephraim.

---

**Q.** Every summer the *Salt Lake Tribune* sponsors what tennis tournament?

**A.** No Champs Tennis Tournament.

**Q.** Where is the Tintic Mining Museum?

**A.** Eureka.

---

**Q.** In what year did the University of Utah first field a football team?

**A.** 1892.

---

**Q.** What museum and visitors center includes the town's historic jail that once held several of the nation's early labor leaders?

**A.** Park City Museum.

---

**Q.** What is Utah's oldest golf course?

**A.** Forest Dale.

---

**Q.** BYU banned what sport for two decades in the early twentieth century?

**A.** Football.

---

**Q.** How long is the Mount Carmel Tunnel, an engineering marvel in Zion National Park?

**A.** 1.1 miles.

---

**Q.** What town hall features a glockenspiel on its front gable?

**A.** Midway.

**Q.** What is considered Utah's most dangerous location for river rafting?

**A.** Cataract Canyon.

---

**Q.** Runners in the *Deseret News* Marathon follow what course?

**A.** Much of the 1847 pioneer route into the Salt Lake Valley.

---

**Q.** The Salt Lake Buzz is a farm team for what major league baseball club?

**A.** Minnesota Twins.

---

**Q.** Widely played by school girls when introduced in Utah, what sport was first thought to be primarily a girls' game?

**A.** Basketball.

---

**Q.** Who was the first BYU football player named All-American?

**A.** Eldon Fortie (1961).

---

**Q.** What city hosts the Huntsman World Senior Games?

**A.** Saint George.

---

**Q.** From the 1880s to the 1930s, the popular Castilla Hot Springs resort was in what location?

**A.** Spanish Fork Canyon.

**Q.** What race car driver achieved a speed of 601 miles per hour on the Bonneville Salt Flats in 1965?

**A.** Craig Breedlove.

**Q.** How many teams are in the expanded Western Athletic Conference (WAC)?

**A.** Sixteen.

**Q.** What South High School and semipro pitcher went directly to the major leagues?

**A.** Kent Peterson.

**Q.** Approximately how many children participated in summer dramatics classes offered by Provo City's WPA recreation program during the Great Depression?

**A.** Four thousand.

**Q.** What natural feature in Zion National Park gets its name from elaborate cable works that lowered timber to the canyon floor?

**A.** Cable Mountain.

**Q.** Dixie College hosts what junior college bowl game in December?

**A.** Dixie Rotary Bowl.

**Q.** What three-time All-American track star at BYU ran in the 220-yard hurdles in Berlin in the 1936 Olympics?

**A.** Dale Schofield.

**Q.** The University of Utah basketball team won the National AAU championship in what year?

**A.** 1916.

—◆—

**Q.** What athletic club, still going strong, was organized in 1912 near Second South and Tenth East in Salt Lake City?

**A.** Salt Lake Tennis Club.

—◆—

**Q.** What former high school and college athletic star served simultaneously as head coach of both football and basketball at Utah State Agricultural College from 1920 until 1941?

**A.** E. L. "Dick" Romney.

—◆—

**Q.** What Utah Sports Hall of Fame bowler first bowled in a tent in Manti in 1899?

**A.** Perc Jensen.

—◆—

**Q.** What Grantsville athlete was named All-American in football in 1933 at the University of Utah?

**A.** Jack Johnson.

—◆—

**Q.** In what canyon are the Brighton and Solitude ski resorts?

**A.** Big Cottonwood.

—◆—

**Q.** What sports arena reportedly had the fastest bicycle racing track in the world in the early twentieth century?

**A.** Salt Palace (the original one).

**Q.** Who was named the NBA Defensive Player of the Year in 1988 and 1989?

**A.** Mark Eaton.

---

**Q.** Utah contains how many national monuments?

**A.** Seven: Dinosaur, Natural Bridges, Rainbow Bridge, Hovenweep, Cedar Breaks, Timpanogos Cave, and the Grand Staircase-Escalante.

---

**Q.** What pass in football was called the "Utah" pass after it was used by the University of Utah against Army in 1957?

**A.** Shovel pass.

---

**Q.** What is the current use for the miners' hospital building erected in Park City in the early 1900s?

**A.** Public library.

---

**Q.** Nate Galloway, a trapper and perhaps a poacher, is believed to have been the first man to perform what feat?

**A.** Run the Green and Colorado Rivers alone.

---

**Q.** What national title did the University of Utah basketball team win in 1947?

**A.** NIT (National Invitational Tournament).

---

**Q.** Where is the National Institute of Fitness?

**A.** Ivins.

**Q.** What ski champion, whose career ended at age eighteen after an accident at Alta in 1955 paralyzed her, was a model of courage as she pursued her dream of becoming a school teacher?

**A.** Jill Kinmont.

———◆———

**Q.** Designed by architect Frederick A. Hale, the clubhouse of what golf course was rebuilt and reopened in 1996?

**A.** Forest Dale.

———◆———

**Q.** What community holds a Lamb Day festival?

**A.** Fountain Green.

———◆———

**Q.** Who was the first coach of the Utah Jazz?

**A.** Tom Nissalke.

———◆———

**Q.** What ski resort town is also the highest municipality in Utah, at 9,850 feet?

**A.** Brian Head.

———◆———

**Q.** Where is the Vic Braden Tennis College?

**A.** Green Valley Resort, Saint George.

———◆———

**Q.** When was the first known game of chess played by telephone in Utah?

**A.** 1881 (between players in Ogden and Salt Lake City).

**Q.** In what sport were the Occidentals, an African-American team, declared the undisputed state champions in 1909 by the *Salt Lake Tribune*?

**A.** Baseball.

---

**Q.** What high Wasatch summit did Albert Carrington, John Brown, and William W. Rust reach on August 21, 1847?

**A.** Twin Peaks.

---

**Q.** What was Utah's first planned resort community with homes, condos, and recreation facilities, including a golf course?

**A.** Bloomington, south of Saint George.

---

**Q.** What town on Bear Lake is a starting point for many snow-mobile trails?

**A.** Garden City.

---

**Q.** The Utah Grizzlies professional hockey team plays in what league?

**A.** International Hockey League.

---

**Q.** Some of the best canoeing locations in the state are in what area?

**A.** Cache Valley.

---

**Q.** The Germania Athletic Club, organized in November 1927, fielded a team in what sport until the late 1970s?

**A.** Soccer.

**Q.** Which northern Utah ski area has been family operated since 1939?

**A.** Beaver Mountain.

---

**Q.** What shelter common in central Asia is used by back-country ski-touring outfitters on overnight trips?

**A.** A yurt (a circular, domed, portable tent).

---

**Q.** Where can scuba divers in Utah see tropical fish?

**A.** Scuba Diving Park at Belmont Springs near Plymouth.

---

**Q.** Who was the first Utah native named to an All-American first team at quarterback?

**A.** Gifford Nielsen.

---

**Q.** Who founded the Utah High School Activities Association in 1910 and was later known as "the father of organized high school athletics"?

**A.** James E. Moss.

---

**Q.** What track star set a world record for the 220-yard dash on a curved track that remained unbroken for thirty-six years until bested by Jesse Owens?

**A.** Creed Haymond.

---

**Q.** What program, the only one like it in North America, lets skiers experience runs at four or five major resorts in one day with back-country guide service between areas?

**A.** Interconnect Adventure Tour.

**Q.** To which Nevada town do "fun" buses from Salt Lake City make daily runs?

**A.** Wendover.

---

**Q.** In what sport did Budd Shields, born in Stockton, Tooele County, set NCAA records in 1928 and 1929?

**A.** Swimming (220- and 440-yard freestyle).

---

**Q.** What was former Olympic athlete Denise Parker's sport?

**A.** Archery.

---

**Q.** What is the number-one tourist attraction in Utah?

**A.** Temple Square.

---

**Q.** What colorful Yugoslavian starred at center on the BYU basketball team in the 1970s and later led his country to an Olympic gold medal?

**A.** Kresimir Cosic.

---

**Q.** What position did softball star Naomi Gatherum Allington play for twenty-five years?

**A.** Pitcher.

---

**Q.** What popular resort hotel in Ogden Canyon was destroyed by fire?

**A.** The Hermitage.

**Q.** What Salt Lake City woman was the World Cup freestyle skiing champion in 1979 and 1980?

**A.** Jan Bucher.

———◆———

**Q.** Which mayor of Salt Lake City set land speed records on the Salt Flats in his Mormon Meteor race car?

**A.** Ab Jenkins.

———◆———

**Q.** Where is the Eccles Dinosaur Park?

**A.** Ogden.

———◆———

**Q.** What former Bear River High and Utah State University athlete won the silver medal in discus throwing at the 1972 Olympic Games?

**A.** Jay Silvester.

———◆———

**Q.** In which park are the International Peace Gardens?

**A.** Jordan.

———◆———

**Q.** What is Salt Lake City's largest hotel?

**A.** Little America (850 rooms).

———◆———

**Q.** In which sport was W. E. "Billy" Samuelson of Provo a top contender in the early twentieth century?

**A.** Bicycle racing.

**Q.** Which NBA team chose University of Utah basketball star Danny Vranes as its number-one draft pick in 1981?

**A.** Seattle SuperSonics.

---

**Q.** Why do thousands of Utahns travel to Franklin, Idaho?

**A.** To buy Idaho lottery tickets.

---

**Q.** Raised in Fort Duchesne, what Utahn was the world featherweight boxing champion from 1976 to 1980?

**A.** Danny Lopez.

---

**Q.** What air carrier offers over 170 daily flights from Salt Lake City to 222 cities worldwide?

**A.** Delta Air Lines.

---

**Q.** Who began a twenty-five-year career as University of Utah athletic director and football coach in 1925?

**A.** Ike Armstrong.

---

**Q.** In 1928 Thomas Caldwell Adams reestablished what boating organization?

**A.** Great Salt Lake Yacht Club.

---

**Q.** Where was Utah's first bungee jumping center?

**A.** Sports Tower, near Logan.

**Q.** What kind of races are held in Wasatch Mountain State Park in February?

**A.** Sled dog races.

———◆———

**Q.** How many cab companies provide taxi service in Salt Lake City?

**A.** Three (City Cab, Ute Cab, and Yellow Cab).

———◆———

**Q.** On the site of what historic ballpark was Franklin Quest Field in Salt Lake City built?

**A.** Derks Field.

———◆———

**Q.** Delta High School's athletic teams have what animal mascot?

**A.** Rabbits.

———◆———

**Q.** What city hosted the first Chautauqua in Utah in July 1911?

**A.** Ogden.

———◆———

**Q.** What kind of event is the Lehi Round-up?

**A.** Rodeo.

———◆———

**Q.** What ethnic group was known for its coffeehouses, especially in the early twentieth century?

**A.** Greeks.

**Q.** BYU defeated what school with a Hail Mary pass from Jim McMahon to Clay Brown in the 1980 Holiday Bowl?

**A.** Southern Methodist University.

◆

**Q.** What high school has fielded a football team since 1893?

**A.** West High School (Salt Lake High School).

◆

**Q.** How many buildings designated Salt Palace, housing sports and other activities in Salt Lake City, preceded the one completed in 1996?

**A.** Two.

◆

**Q.** What town celebrates Golden Onion Days in September?

**A.** Payson.

◆

**Q.** Which high school football team was once called the Smelterites?

**A.** Tooele High School.

◆

**Q.** What was former Olympic athlete Suzy Harris Rytting's sport?

**A.** Skiing.

◆

**Q.** What was "Old Ironsides," which was mounted on the *Salt Lake Tribune* Building each fall from 1915 to 1957?

**A.** Electric scoreboard for the World Series.

**Q.** What woman in the Utah Golf Hall of Fame won the Utah State Amateur Championship eight times during 1955–79 and more than fifty other victories?

**A.** Bev Nelson.

———◆———

**Q.** Which high school was the first to install lights for night football games?

**A.** East High School (1943).

———◆———

**Q.** What town is known for its fine equestrian park and its historic Old Rock Church?

**A.** Parowan.

———◆———

**Q.** Venues for seven events at the 2002 Winter Olympics—slalom, giant slalom, freestyle aerials, ski jump, Nordic combined, and luge—will be in which county?

**A.** Summit.

———◆———

**Q.** What successful brewery owner in Ogden was also one of the world's best trapshooters?

**A.** Gustav Becker.

———◆———

**Q.** Ike Armstrong coached what sport at the University of Utah?

**A.** Football.

———◆———

**Q.** What Wasatch County town hosts an annual Swiss Days festival?

**A.** Midway.

**Q.** Near which national park did Reuben Syrett open Ruby's Inn in 1920?

**A.** Bryce Canyon.

---

**Q.** For which sport did M. H. Walker, a wealthy Salt Lake City businessman, organize and host the first known tournament in June 1885?

**A.** Tennis.

---

**Q.** Missy Marlowe starred in what sport at the University of Utah?

**A.** Gymnastics.

---

**Q.** Who was the first general manager, and later coach, of the Utah Jazz?

**A.** Frank Layden.

---

**Q.** What site in Provo Canyon boasts one of the world's steepest trams to take viewers to an overlook?

**A.** Bridal Veil Falls.

---

**Q.** Teams from Eureka and Fort Douglas played the first known game of what sport in Utah in October 1869?

**A.** Baseball.

---

**Q.** Stan Watts coached what sport at Brigham Young University?

**A.** Basketball.

**Q.** What place of leisure activity did Salt Lake City officials buy in 1865 in order to supervise it more closely?

**A.** A "billiard saloon."

——————◆——————

**Q.** Which state park includes a twenty-seven-hole golf course?

**A.** Wasatch Mountain.

——————◆——————

**Q.** What Parowan farm boy won a gold medal—the first for a Utahn—in high jumping at the 1912 Olympic Games in Stockholm?

**A.** Alma Richards.

——————◆——————

**Q.** Besides Salt Lake City, what other Utah town fielded baseball teams in the Pioneer League?

**A.** Ogden.

——————◆——————

**Q.** In the 1880s one of Utah's early dance halls was built in a cave in which canyon?

**A.** American Fork.

——————◆——————

**Q.** What young boy, who later became a famous boxer, dropped out of the eighth grade in Provo and began riding the rails around the West, picking up fights in mining camps?

**A.** Jack Dempsey.

——————◆——————

**Q.** What is the largest ski area in the state, with thirteen lifts, a gondola, and eighty-nine trails?

**A.** Park City.

**Q.** What turn-of-the-century steam train takes visitors into Provo Canyon?

**A.** "Heber Creeper," or Heber Valley Historic Railroad.

◆

**Q.** Spencer D. "Sparky" Adams, the first known Utah native to play major league baseball, was born and raised in what town?

**A.** Layton.

◆

**Q.** What was the Wolf Mountain ski area previously called?

**A.** Park West.

◆

**Q.** Visitors to the McCurdy Museum in Provo expect to see what toys?

**A.** Dolls.

◆

**Q.** The Heber City airport is used by pilots of what small aircraft?

**A.** Gliders.

◆

**Q.** What NFL quarterback is a direct descendant of pioneer leader Brigham Young?

**A.** Steve Young.

◆

**Q.** What form of transportation takes adventuresome cross-country skiers to remote areas for powder skiing?

**A.** Helicopter.

**Q.** What Utah town has become internationally known to mountain-biking enthusiasts?

**A.** Moab.

———◆———

**Q.** What former Salt Lake City women's softball team, perennial state champions, took second place in the world championships in 1953?

**A.** Utah Shamrocks.

———◆———

**Q.** Steel Days is associated with which city in Utah County?

**A.** American Fork.

———◆———

**Q.** What Utah State University and L.A. Rams defensive lineman was named to the Pro Football Hall of Fame in 1982?

**A.** Merlin Olsen.

———◆———

**Q.** What Norwegian native pioneered ski jumping in Utah and is the only person to have placed first in all four skiing events—downhill, slalom, jumping, and cross-country—at a national championship competition?

**A.** Alf Engen.

———◆———

**Q.** At which national monument do visitors walk through the Cavern of Sleep and the Father Time Jewel Box?

**A.** Timpanogos Cave.

———◆———

**Q.** Georgie White, an active commercial guide into her seventies, helped pioneer what popular outdoor activity?

**A.** River running.

**Q.** What professional golfer, winner of the U.S. Open in 1973 and the British Open in 1976, starred on BYU's golf team in the 1960s?

**A.** Johnny Miller.

◆

**Q.** Which national forest in Utah has more recreational use than any other national forest in America?

**A.** Wasatch-Cache National Forest.

◆

**Q.** "Poosh 'Em Up" Tony Lazzeri played for what Utah team before starring with the Ruth-era New York Yankees?

**A.** Salt Lake Bees.

◆

**Q.** A pioneer village, opera house, and water park are part of what large amusement park?

**A.** Lagoon.

◆

**Q.** Harry L. Aleson is believed to have been the first man to make a living from what popular boating activity?

**A.** River running.

◆

**Q.** What Utah woman golfer defeated the legendary Mildred "Babe" Didriksen Zaharias in a 1938 match?

**A.** Helen Hofmann Bertagnole.

◆

**Q.** What BLM area west of Nephi is a favorite of off-road vehicle users because of its shifting sand dunes?

**A.** Little Sahara Recreation Area.

# SCIENCE & NATURE

## C H A P T E R    S I X

**Q.** What did a famous seismologist's study of the 1934 Hansel Valley earthquake help him devise?

**A.** Richter Scale (Charles F. Richter).

**Q.** What predator is responsible for the most sheep-lamb kills in Utah?

**A.** Coyote.

**Q.** What rare tree is found in the Twisted Forest near Brian Head?

**A.** Bristlecone pine.

**Q.** What is increased rain or snowfall called when storms pick up added moisture from passing over Great Salt Lake?

**A.** Lake effect precipitation.

**Q.** What prehistoric culture covering much of present Utah was first identified in 1931 by Harvard anthropologist Noel Morss?

**A.** Fremont Culture.

**Q.** What Utah company produces solid fuel motors for missiles and booster rockets for spacecraft?

**A.** Thiokol.

———◆———

**Q.** What tropical fish food is harvested in the Great Salt Lake?

**A.** Brine shrimp.

———◆———

**Q.** Chemists Stanley Pons and Martin Fleischman made what controversial announcement on March 23, 1989?

**A.** They had achieved cold fusion.

———◆———

**Q.** Twenty-two thousand pounds of what Utah food product was shipped to a Chicago dealer from Springville on November 3, 1892?

**A.** Honey.

———◆———

**Q.** What did well diggers in Leamington, Millard County, claim to have unearthed in January 1889 as part of a hoax?

**A.** A petrified human head.

———◆———

**Q.** An epidemic of what disease, causing 188 illnesses and 13 deaths, was traced to a Salt Lake City delicatessen worker in 1923?

**A.** Typhoid fever.

———◆———

**Q.** What scientist is the only person to have served as president of both Utah State University, when it was Utah State Agricultural College, and the University of Utah?

**A.** John A. Widtsoe.

**Q.** What are the general dimensions of the Great Salt Lake?

**A.** Thirty miles wide and eighty miles long.

———◆———

**Q.** Approximately how many dead flies did the winner of a "swat the fly" contest deliver to health officials to win a one-thousand-dollar prize at the turn of the century?

**A.** 9.5 million.

———◆———

**Q.** Between which two major migratory bird routes do the marshes of Great Salt Lake lie?

**A.** Pacific and Central Flyways.

———◆———

**Q.** What kind of system begun by R. T. Porte in Salt Lake City in 1917 revolutionized the printing industry worldwide?

**A.** Price estimating.

———◆———

**Q.** What national youth organization were Boys Potato Growing Clubs the forerunners of in Utah in the early 1900s?

**A.** 4-H Club.

———◆———

**Q.** Beginning in the mid-1890s, what natural product was harvested on Gunnison Island?

**A.** Guano.

———◆———

**Q.** Vaccination for which communicable disease was hotly debated in Utah in the late-nineteenth and early-twentieth centuries?

**A.** Smallpox.

**Q.** What fossils, found in large numbers in the House Range of Millard County by members of the Wheeler Survey in the 1870s, were not rediscovered until the 1920s, when Frank Beckwith came across them?

**A.** Trilobites.

---

**Q.** How many head of livestock were handled by the Ogden stockyards in 1926?

**A.** Almost 1.5 million.

---

**Q.** What bird on the endangered species list has sometimes nested on downtown Salt Lake City buildings in recent years?

**A.** Peregrine falcon.

---

**Q.** Who was the first professionally trained archaeologist to work in Utah?

**A.** Neil Judd.

---

**Q.** In 1920 Utah was the leading producer in the United States of what breed of sheep?

**A.** Rambouillet.

---

**Q.** What general health precaution did Salt Lake City officials inaugurate in 1915?

**A.** Chlorination of water.

---

**Q.** In what city did Incarnacion Florez develop a large following as a *curandera,* or healer?

**A.** Salt Lake City.

**Q.** By the 1920s what Utah inventor and manufacturer had created an international market for his radio receivers and headsets?

**A.** Nathaniel Baldwin.

———◆———

**Q.** In September 1944 the BYU horticultural department claimed to have grown under normal field conditions tomatoes weighing how many pounds each?

**A.** Four.

———◆———

**Q.** What Utah industry was devastated by the assassination of John F. Kennedy?

**A.** Turkey processing (because of the president's death on November 22, 1963, many Americans did not prepare elaborate turkey dinners on Thanksgiving).

———◆———

**Q.** What can visitors to Parowan Gap see?

**A.** Some of Utah's best petroglyphs.

———◆———

**Q.** The Road Creek Ranch in Loa markets what gourmet food product?

**A.** Smoked trout fillets.

———◆———

**Q.** Green River is noted for what type of fruit?

**A.** Melons.

———◆———

**Q.** What remedy for internal bleeding did G. D. Watt advertise in 1851?

**A.** Blood stone.

**Q.** Why was John Hill shot and killed near Wellsville in 1863?

**A.** He was mistaken for a bear.

———◆———

**Q.** What kind of mushroom weighing 11.25 pounds did Salt Lake City businessman Wayne Decker find in August 1934 near Oakley?

**A.** Puffball.

———◆———

**Q.** In 1982 Thomas D. Dee II endowed a chair at the University of Utah in which scientific discipline?

**A.** Medical genetics.

———◆———

**Q.** Where can wild horses, including rare, distinctively marked descendants of early Spanish Tarpan mounts, be seen?

**A.** West of Cedar City in the Bureau of Land Management's Sulphur Wild Horse Management Area.

———◆———

**Q.** What kind of "patients" received care in the hospital opened in 1894 by the Charles H. King family?

**A.** Dolls.

———◆———

**Q.** What rare animal was seen in the Ashley National Forest north of Vernal in the early 1940s?

**A.** A white deer.

———◆———

**Q.** What Utah home economist and college professor was named a distinguished professor of home sciences at the University of Ghana in 1967?

**A.** Virginia F. Cutler.

**Q.** What was unique about the silver deposits at Silver Reef?

**A.** The silver was found in sandstone.

———◆———

**Q.** What is Utah-based Dynix?

**A.** The world's leading library automation company.

———◆———

**Q.** Who founded one of the largest private ranches in Utah in Nine Mile Canyon in 1902?

**A.** Preston Nutter.

———◆———

**Q.** Upon its completion in 1914, what world engineering marvel did a Utah realtor advertise would stimulate a large influx of European immigrants to the West Coast and on to Utah?

**A.** Panama Canal.

———◆———

**Q.** What unusual dinosaur was found by Smithsonian Institution scientists on North Horn Mountain in Emery County in 1937?

**A.** Titanosaur.

———◆———

**Q.** What unit of Zion National Park, added in 1956, is overlooked by most of the millions who visit the park?

**A.** Kolob Canyons.

———◆———

**Q.** What Farmington businesswoman and philanthropist also delivered 3,977 babies during her long career as a midwife?

**A.** Patty Bartlett Sessions.

**Q.** Remains of what large prehistoric animal, along with projectile points, were found near Huntington Reservoir in 1988?

**A.** Mammoth.

---

**Q.** Critical habitats have been designated in southern Utah for what threatened reptile?

**A.** Desert tortoise.

---

**Q.** In what year did equipment for making regular meteorological readings arrive in Utah from the Smithsonian Institution?

**A.** 1857.

---

**Q.** What former U.S. president was awestruck at the sight of Rainbow Bridge in the moonlight on a 1913 visit to the national monument?

**A.** Theodore Roosevelt.

---

**Q.** What was the target area for Athena and Pershing missiles test fired from the Utah Launch Complex near Green River?

**A.** White Sands Missile Range, New Mexico.

---

**Q.** What privately owned cave near Gandy in west Millard County is said to rival Lehman Caves in Great Basin National Park in terms of size and variety of formations?

**A.** Crystal Cave, also called Crystal Ball Cave.

---

**Q.** In the 1880s Frank E. McGurrin, an employee of the Third District Court, was reported to be the fastest person in the world at what skill?

**A.** Typing.

**Q.** What farming technique did David Broadhead discover was suited to the sloping foothills of Levan Ridge, Juab County?

**A.** Dry farming.

———◆———

**Q.** What tree did early white settlers often call cedar?

**A.** Utah juniper.

———◆———

**Q.** What scientific breakthrough did BYU microbiologist Scott Woodward make in 1994?

**A.** Extracted DNA from dinosaur bone.

———◆———

**Q.** What do the Oquirrh Mountains lack that the Wasatch Mountains have in abundance?

**A.** Large ever-flowing streams.

———◆———

**Q.** In 1993 Utah led the United States in the production of what animal product?

**A.** Mink pelts.

———◆———

**Q.** In 1895 Dr. William H. Groves left an estate valued at seventy-five thousand dollars to be used for what purpose?

**A.** To build LDS Hospital.

———◆———

**Q.** Big Red is the nickname for what river?

**A.** Colorado.

**Q.** What unusual animal decoy made by Indians was donated to the Deseret Museum in 1880?

**A.** Pronghorn antelope.

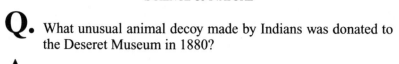

**Q.** What is the popular name of a spectacular fifteen-hundred-foot feature of Canyonlands National Park that geologists think is either a collapsed salt dome or a meteorite impact crater?

**A.** Upheaval Dome.

**Q.** To what Utah city did HawkWatch International, founded in 1986 in New Mexico, relocate its offices in 1993?

**A.** Salt Lake City.

**Q.** The construction of which interstate led to the discovery of the largest known village of the Fremont Culture?

**A.** Interstate 70 in Clear Creek Canyon.

**Q.** What is the largest no-kill animal sanctuary in the United States?

**A.** Best Friends Animal Sanctuary in Kanab Canyon.

**Q.** Who was the second Utahn, after Brigham Young, to be represented in Statuary Hall in the U.S. Capitol?

**A.** Philo T. Farnsworth, "the Father of Television."

**Q.** What large raptors are year-round residents of the Ouray National Wildlife Refuge?

**A.** Golden eagles.

**Q.** What is the greatest depth of the Great Salt Lake?

**A.** Thirty-two feet.

———◆———

**Q.** What did Earl Douglass discover in Uintah County in August 1909?

**A.** Dinosaur fossils.

———◆———

**Q.** What body of water is one of the most prolific producers of Mackinaw trout weighing over thirty pounds?

**A.** Flaming Gorge Reservoir.

———◆———

**Q.** How many years did it take to build the six-mile Duchesne Tunnel through a mountain to convey water from the Duchesne River to the Provo River drainage system?

**A.** Twelve years.

———◆———

**Q.** What religious denomination opened the first hospital in Utah in 1872?

**A.** Episcopal (Saint Mark's Hospital).

———◆———

**Q.** Where is Utah's only fire tower, which is listed in the National Register of Historic Places?

**A.** South of Manila, Ute Mountain Fire Tower.

———◆———

**Q.** For what well-known Utah geologist was the dinosaur *Stokesosaurus clevelandi* named?

**A.** William L. Stokes.

**Q.** For what did Brigham Young receive a twenty-five-dollar prize at an 1856 fair?

**A.** Stud horse.

◆

**Q.** In the production of what four fruits was Utah ranked among the top ten states in a 1995 report?

**A.** Tart cherry (second), apricot (third), sweet cherry (fifth), pear (ninth).

◆

**Q.** What do autumn buttercup, dwarf bear poppy, and Kodachrome bladderpod—all found in Utah—have in common?

**A.** All are endangered plant species.

◆

**Q.** What important hydrocarbon is named for a former pony express rider, U.S. marshal, and prospector?

**A.** Gilsonite (for Sam Gilson).

◆

**Q.** How many tons of dinosaur bones from Utah had been shipped to the Carnegie Museum in Pittsburgh by 1924?

**A.** More than 350.

◆

**Q.** What was the name of the famous lion-tiger cross at Hogle Zoological Gardens, now mounted and on display at the zoo?

**A.** Shasta.

◆

**Q.** Billionaire Jon M. Huntsman has generously funded scientific research in what area at the University of Utah?

**A.** Cancer.

**Q.** What breed of dog was used to herd sheep on Antelope Island in 1873?

**A.** Saint Bernard.

◆

**Q.** What men's fashion item led to the colorful era of the mountain men and fur trappers?

**A.** Beaver hats.

◆

**Q.** After having been hunted almost to extinction, what member of the deer family was successfully reintroduced into Utah in 1912?

**A.** Elk.

◆

**Q.** Which county is the state's leading producer of hay?

**A.** Millard.

◆

**Q.** How many seeds did "the great pumpkin" displayed in ZCMI's window in 1894 contain?

**A.** 574.

◆

**Q.** A monument in Huntsville is dedicated to Mary Heathman "Granny" Smith for what community service?

**A.** Serving as the community's doctor, nurse, and midwife (delivering some fifteen hundred babies).

◆

**Q.** What destructive insect was first observed in Salt Lake City in 1988?

**A.** Gypsy moth.

**Q.** What county had the greatest number of cattle in 1995?

**A.** Box Elder.

---

**Q.** What fruit is especially associated with Bear Lake?

**A.** Raspberries.

---

**Q.** In 1856 John M. Wooley won what competition sponsored by the Deseret Agriculture and Manufacturing Society?

**A.** Plowing match.

---

**Q.** What rodent found in the Wasatch and Uinta Ranges can glide through the air?

**A.** Flying squirrel.

---

**Q.** A large cooperative venture established in the 1990s in the Milford area raises what farm product?

**A.** Hogs.

---

**Q.** What is the tallest water bird in Utah?

**A.** Great blue heron (about three feet tall).

---

**Q.** What engineering marvel did the Southern Pacific Railroad complete across the Great Salt Lake in 1903?

**A.** Lucin Cutoff.

**Q.** What county leads the state in dairy production?

**A.** Cache.

———◆———

**Q.** In 1872 cars of the Salt Lake City Street Railway system were moved by what power source?

**A.** Mules.

———◆———

**Q.** What winged creatures are exhibited in a walk-through natural setting as one of Hogle Zoological Gardens' newest attractions?

**A.** Butterflies.

———◆———

**Q.** Utah wool growers annually lose on average what percentage of their flocks to predators?

**A.** 10 percent.

———◆———

**Q.** What metropolitan area receives the largest percentage of electricity generated by the Intermountain Power plant near Delta?

**A.** Los Angeles.

———◆———

**Q.** What marsh plant used by Native Americans can reportedly produce thousands of pounds of flour per acre annually?

**A.** Cattails.

———◆———

**Q.** Why do foresters consider the porcupine a pest?

**A.** It often kills trees by gnawing away a ring of bark.

**Q.** Two large dioramas of Utah bird life on the Great Salt Lake were once featured by what museum in a neighboring state?

**A.** Denver Museum of Natural History.

——————◆——————

**Q.** Rocky Mountain spotted fever is transmitted by what insect?

**A.** Wood tick.

——————◆——————

**Q.** What high post in a U.S. Department of Agriculture agency did Edward P. Cliff, a Heber City native, attain in 1962?

**A.** Chief forester of the United States.

——————◆——————

**Q.** Which state park has an annual roundup of bison?

**A.** Antelope Island.

——————◆——————

**Q.** What feat brought international fame to pilot Russell L. Maughan of Cache County on June 21, 1925?

**A.** First nonstop dawn-to-dusk flight from New York to San Francisco.

——————◆——————

**Q.** Which ethnic group successfully introduced labor-intensive cash crops such as cauliflower and cabbage into Sanpete County in the 1920s?

**A.** Japanese.

——————◆——————

**Q.** For two years Marvel Lay Murdock of Heber City and Duchesne served as president of what national organization?

**A.** National Women's Auxiliary of the National Wool Growers Association.

**Q.** What is Utah's state tree?

**A.** Blue spruce.

———◆———

**Q.** What is the average annual snowfall in inches at Alta, Brighton, Powder Mountain, and Snowbird ski resorts?

**A.** Five hundred.

———◆———

**Q.** What international health and beauty product line, with some 370,000 distributors in Asia, is based in Provo?

**A.** Nu-Skin International.

———◆———

**Q.** What Wasatch County native was a key prosecution witness in the Lindbergh case, identifying Bruno Hauptmann's handwriting on a ransom note?

**A.** James Clark Sellers.

———◆———

**Q.** In what classification does the Utah Department of Agriculture place dyers woad, hoary cress, and Russian thistle?

**A.** Noxious weeds.

———◆———

**Q.** In what year did state governors first meet, in Utah, to discuss conservation of natural resources?

**A.** 1908.

———◆———

**Q.** What nickname was given to Ibapah rancher Elizabeth Dunlop Ferguson Bonnemort?

**A.** Sheep Queen.

**Q.** In what year was natural gas first available for Salt Lake City residences?

**A.** 1929.

———◆———

**Q.** Water from which reservoir was first delivered to Salt Lake City users in 1955?

**A.** Deer Creek.

———◆———

**Q.** What is the largest manmade excavation on earth?

**A.** Kennecott's Bingham Canyon Mine.

———◆———

**Q.** What bird is featured on Utah's state seal?

**A.** Eagle.

———◆———

**Q.** What is America's only public bird park displaying more than one thousand birds?

**A.** Tracy Aviary.

———◆———

**Q.** What pioneering work did Lucien L. Nunn and Paul Nunn do at the electric power plant in Provo Canyon?

**A.** Production and transmission of alternating current.

———◆———

**Q.** Which mining district in Utah produced more gold than the Mother Lode District in Calaveras County, California?

**A.** Tintic (2.6 million ounces to 2 million ounces).

**Q.** At what living-history dairy farm in Salt lake City can visitors experience farm life of the 1890s?

**A.** Wheeler Historic Farm.

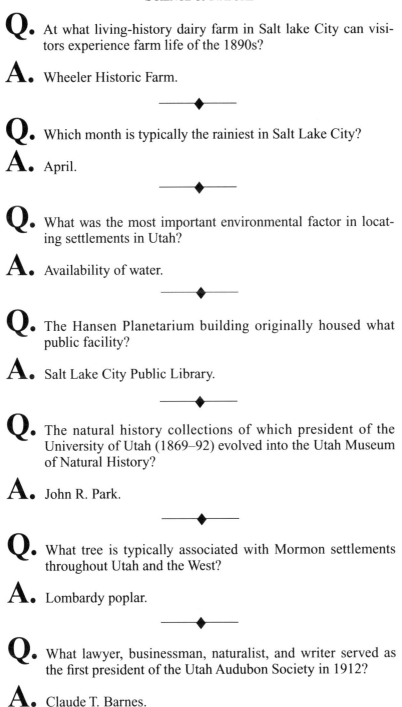

**Q.** Which month is typically the rainiest in Salt Lake City?

**A.** April.

**Q.** What was the most important environmental factor in locating settlements in Utah?

**A.** Availability of water.

**Q.** The Hansen Planetarium building originally housed what public facility?

**A.** Salt Lake City Public Library.

**Q.** The natural history collections of which president of the University of Utah (1869–92) evolved into the Utah Museum of Natural History?

**A.** John R. Park.

**Q.** What tree is typically associated with Mormon settlements throughout Utah and the West?

**A.** Lombardy poplar.

**Q.** What lawyer, businessman, naturalist, and writer served as the first president of the Utah Audubon Society in 1912?

**A.** Claude T. Barnes.

**Q.** What is Utah's official state fossil?

**A.** *Allosaurus.*

---

**Q.** In Utah farming communities, a ditchrider worked under whose supervision?

**A.** Watermaster.

---

**Q.** Where was the first federally funded reclamation project in Utah?

**A.** Strawberry Valley (reservoir authorized in 1905).

---

**Q.** What museum has one of the largest collections of vintage aircraft and ordnance in the United States?

**A.** Hill Aerospace.

---

**Q.** Although it is not a native species, what fish that thrives in Utah waters was named the official state fish in 1971?

**A.** Rainbow trout.

---

**Q.** What is the common name of the very common Utah plant species *Artemisia*?

**A.** Sagebrush.

---

**Q.** What popular mythical creature with the body of a jackrabbit and the horns of a small antelope is often found in Utah souvenir shops?

**A.** Jackalope.

**Q.** What name is given to southern Utahns who were exposed to high levels of radiation during nuclear weapons testing in the 1950s and 1960s?

**A.** Downwinders.

———◆———

**Q.** The third attempt in the United States to televise an operation for doctors to witness took place in February 1949 in which hospital?

**A.** LDS Hospital.

———◆———

**Q.** What is Utah's state bird?

**A.** California gull.

———◆———

**Q.** Which member of the Young family opened the Salt Lake City Museum and Menagerie, which later became the Deseret Museum?

**A.** John W. Young.

———◆———

**Q.** Which Brigham Young University scientist founded the *Great Basin Naturalist* in 1939 and edited thirty volumes of it?

**A.** Vasco M. Tanner.

———◆———

**Q.** Salt Lake Valley farmers sued what industry in 1904 and 1906, claiming crop losses from pollution?

**A.** Smelting.

———◆———

**Q.** During 1880–82 there was a medical college in what small northern Utah town?

**A.** Morgan.

**Q.** Which Utah scientist pioneered the study of agriculture in dry climates?

**A.** John A. Widtsoe.

---

**Q.** What is the general elevation of the Great Salt Lake?

**A.** Forty-two hundred feet.

---

**Q.** What is the number-one carrier of rabies in Utah?

**A.** Bats.

---

**Q.** Which Sanpete County town won the nation's first statewide Clean Town Contest in 1914?

**A.** Manti.

---

**Q.** What institution began as a land-grant agricultural college in 1888?

**A.** Utah State University.

---

**Q.** What body of water is more than five miles long and is 8,843 feet above sea level?

**A.** Fish Lake.

---

**Q.** What Utah product was in great demand in the Butte, Montana, mines for use in ore reduction?

**A.** Salt.

**Q.** During World War II, why were German- and Japanese-style buildings erected at Dugway Proving Grounds?

**A.** For use as targets for various military weapons.

———◆———

**Q.** What University of Utah plant ecologist, known for his study of the effects of grazing on vegetation, has a grove of hybrid oak in Red Butte Canyon named in his honor?

**A.** Walter P. Cottam.

———◆———

**Q.** What is the state gem?

**A.** Topaz.

———◆———

**Q.** Congress established what natural area in northern Utah on April 23, 1928, as a bird refuge?

**A.** Bear River Migratory Bird Refuge.

———◆———

**Q.** What kind of animal was "Big Foot," trapped by Ray Musselman on March 24, 1920, to the relief of ranchers who blamed the beast for large stock losses?

**A.** Wolf.

———◆———

**Q.** What is the official name of the biological science museum at Brigham Young University?

**A.** Monte L. Bean Life Sciences Museum.

———◆———

**Q.** Brought to Utah in 1877 by the Walker brothers, what small bird was so disliked by farmers in the 1880s that a bounty was placed on it?

**A.** English sparrow.

**Q.** What is the state animal?

**A.** Elk.

———◆———

**Q.** At the south end of Elk Ridge, what formation is named for the part of an animal that it resembles?

**A.** Bears Ears.

———◆———

**Q.** What alternative name for the hydrocarbon gilsonite reflects where it was found?

**A.** Uintaite.

———◆———

**Q.** What is the number-one direct weather-related cause of death in Utah?

**A.** Lightning.

———◆———

**Q.** At which national park did Angus M. Woodbury, later a distinguished vertebrate zoologist at the University of Utah, serve in 1925 as the first naturalist?

**A.** Zion National Park.

———◆———

**Q.** What inventor's workshop and weapons can be seen at Union Station in Ogden?

**A.** John M. Browning.

———◆———

**Q.** Gunnison Island in the Great Salt Lake is an important breeding place for which large bird?

**A.** White pelican.

**Q.** What form of public transportation first appeared in Salt Lake City in 1889?

**A.** Electric streetcars.

———◆———

**Q.** Why did Utahns plant some ten thousand mulberry trees in the 1870s?

**A.** To feed silkworms (and therefore increase silk production).

———◆———

**Q.** Who received the world's first artificial heart, at the University of Utah Medical Center?

**A.** Barney Clark.

———◆———

**Q.** What is transhumance, widely practiced in Utah?

**A.** Seasonal movement of livestock from summer to winter ranges.

———◆———

**Q.** What is the state insect?

**A.** Honeybee.

———◆———

**Q.** Stories about what strange "beast" frightened residents along the Utah-Idaho border in 1868?

**A.** Bear Lake Monster.

———◆———

**Q.** Hydraulics—including holes, reversals, rollers, suck holes, and pour-overs—are hazards associated with activity on or in what?

**A.** Rivers.

**Q.** What does Brigham City call its harvest festival, claimed to be the oldest such continuous one in Utah?

**A.** Peach Days.

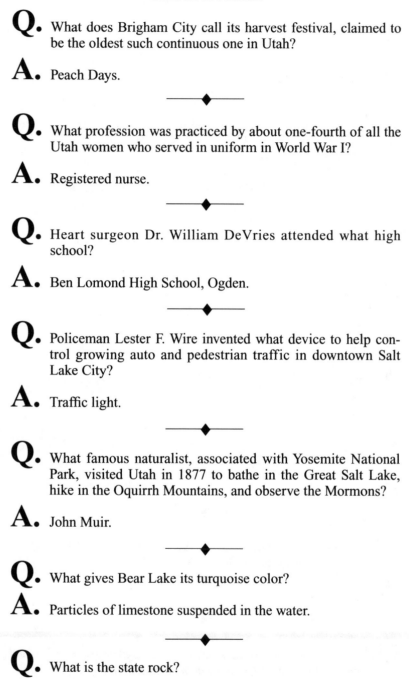

**Q.** What profession was practiced by about one-fourth of all the Utah women who served in uniform in World War I?

**A.** Registered nurse.

**Q.** Heart surgeon Dr. William DeVries attended what high school?

**A.** Ben Lomond High School, Ogden.

**Q.** Policeman Lester F. Wire invented what device to help control growing auto and pedestrian traffic in downtown Salt Lake City?

**A.** Traffic light.

**Q.** What famous naturalist, associated with Yosemite National Park, visited Utah in 1877 to bathe in the Great Salt Lake, hike in the Oquirrh Mountains, and observe the Mormons?

**A.** John Muir.

**Q.** What gives Bear Lake its turquoise color?

**A.** Particles of limestone suspended in the water.

**Q.** What is the state rock?

**A.** Coal.

**Q.** In what geological formation are most dinosaur bones found?

**A.** Morrison Formation.

---

**Q.** What is Utah's best-known example of an entrenched meander?

**A.** Goosenecks of the San Juan River.

---

**Q.** What Utah arch is named for a president of the National Geographic Society?

**A.** Grosvenor Arch (Gilbert Grosvenor).

---

**Q.** What Utah mountain range was named to honor the secretary of the Smithsonian Institution?

**A.** Henry Mountains (Joseph Henry).

---

**Q.** The name of which southern Utah community commemorates an impressive force of nature?

**A.** Hurricane.

---

**Q.** The excavations at Danger Cave were directed by what archaeologist?

**A.** Jesse D. Jennings.

---

**Q.** The 1854 Utah territorial legislature offered a cash prize for the discovery of what important resource?

**A.** Coal within a forty-mile radius of Salt Lake City.

**Q.** Who is considered the father of Utah copper mining?

**A.** Daniel C. Jackling.

———◆———

**Q.** What was the purpose of the project SMART on Hurricane Mesa?

**A.** To test ejection systems for use by air force jet pilots.

———◆———

**Q.** Salt Lake City buildings were first supplied electrical power in what year?

**A.** 1881.

———◆———

**Q.** When was the Flaming Gorge Dam completed?

**A.** 1963.

———◆———

**Q.** What Utahn was the first public official to travel in space?

**A.** Senator Jake Garn in April 1985.

———◆———

**Q.** In what year did waters from flooding City Creek flow down Salt Lake City's State Street?

**A.** 1983.

———◆———

**Q.** How long ago did Utah's geologic history begin?

**A.** More than 2.5 billion years.

**Q.** What are the eastern and western boundaries of the Great Basin?

**A.** The Wasatch Mountains and the Sierra Nevada.

———◆———

**Q.** What three major rivers flow into the Great Salt Lake?

**A.** Jordan, Bear, and Weber.

———◆———

**Q.** The Great Salt Lake is how much saltier than the Pacific Ocean?

**A.** Eight times.

———◆———

**Q.** Who led early archaeological expeditions to the Four Corners area and founded the Department of Archaeology at the University of Utah in 1914?

**A.** Byron Cummings.

———◆———

**Q.** What is the highest percentage of salt in the waters of the Great Salt Lake?

**A.** 27 percent.

———◆———

**Q.** What beekeeper won first place for his honey at the 1903 St. Louis World's Fair?

**A.** Christian Ottesen of Huntington.

———◆———

**Q.** How long is the Jordan River?

**A.** Forty miles.

**Q.** What southern Utah area has created controversy between those favoring coal mining and those against it for conservation and environmental reasons?

**A.** Kaiparowits Plateau.

---

**Q.** When did the Utah Museum of Natural History open?

**A.** 1969.

---

**Q.** When was the first dinosaur discovered in Utah?

**A.** 1877 (by E. D. Cope).

---

**Q.** What is the predominant dinosaur found in the Cleveland-Lloyd Dinosaur Quarry?

**A.** *Allosaurus.*

---

**Q.** What is the elevation of Panguitch?

**A.** 6,666 feet.

---

**Q.** What is Utah's state flower?

**A.** Sego lily.

---

**Q.** The name of a wildflower growing nearby was given to what small Duchesne County agricultural town?

**A.** Bluebell.

**Q.** What is the only county in Utah named for a tree?

**A.** Box Elder.

———◆———

**Q.** What Summit County city was named for an important fuel source found there?

**A.** Coalville.

———◆———

**Q.** What famous landmark in Weber Canyon consists of two vertical, parallel limestone reefs?

**A.** Devil's Slide.

———◆———

**Q.** What Utah County town was named, in an effort to encourage settlement, for a kind of fruit?

**A.** Elberta (peach).

———◆———

**Q.** When a large slab of rock fell, narrowly missing workers, what archeological site, now a state park, received its name?

**A.** Danger Cave.

———◆———

**Q.** What Oquirrh Mountain peak honors the developer of the image dissector, an invention that led to television?

**A.** Farnsworth Peak (Philo T. Farnsworth).

———◆———

**Q.** What high mountain lake in central Utah was an important food source for the Ute Indians?

**A.** Fish Lake.

**Q.** What former associate professor of computer science at Brigham Young University was a cofounder of WordPerfect?

**A.** Alan Ashton.

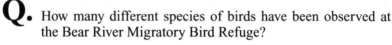

**Q.** What is Utah's most popular place to view elk?

**A.** Hardware Ranch.

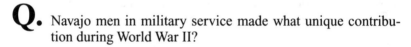

**Q.** How many different species of birds have been observed at the Bear River Migratory Bird Refuge?

**A.** More than two hundred.

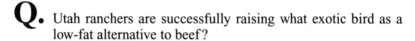

**Q.** Navajo men in military service made what unique contribution during World War II?

**A.** They sent messages in the Navajo language, thus confusing Japanese code breakers.

**Q.** Utah ranchers are successfully raising what exotic bird as a low-fat alternative to beef?

**A.** Ostrich.

**Q.** In which hospital were Siamese twins separated in 1996 after a prolonged series of operations?

**A.** Primary Children's Hospital.